C000185029

Born into a cult

The

Tattooed Saint

KEVIN COCKBURN

In Memory

The Tattooed Saint is in memory of Mr. C (My Dad) and Mo.
Two very special people who passed during the writing of this book.

Dedications

I wish to thank my mum. When it comes to Mum, she is simply next level; the epitome of a powerful, faithful and forgiving life lived. Despite very grave odds, the strength of this lady to survive the life she was subjected to, without an ounce of bitterness, is startling, humbling, and the greatest example to me of a life lived.

THE TATTOOED SAINT
Copyright © 2021 by Kevin Cockburn

ISBN: 978-1-8384838-5-2

All rights reserved.
No part of this publication may be reproduced, stored in a retrieval system, or transmitted in any form or by any means, electronic, mechanical, photocopying or otherwise, without prior written consent of the publisher except as provided by under United Kingdom copyright law. Short extracts may be used for review purposes with credits given.

The ESV® Bible (The Holy Bible, English Standard Version®). ESV® Text Edition: 2016. Copyright © 2001 by Crossway, a publishing ministry of Good News Publishers. The ESV® text has been reproduced in cooperation with and by permission of Good News Publishers. Unauthorized reproduction of this publication is prohibited. All rights reserved.

Published by

Maurice Wylie Media
Your Inspirational Publisher

Publishers' statement: Throughout this book the love for our God is such that whenever we refer to Him we honour with Capitals. On the other hand, when referring to the devil, we refuse to acknowledge him with any honour to the point of violating grammatical rule and withholding capitalisation.

For more information visit
www.MauriceWylieMedia.com

Endorsement

I was born into the same cult as Kevin and only recently published my story as part of a cult awareness campaign called Cult Escape. I was delighted when Kevin told me he was writing his story too. Reading his book brings back the gruesome memories of our coercively controlled past that we are very fortunate to have escaped from.

This is a book you won't be able to put down. It will have you shaking your head with shock, horror and disbelief, to amazement and laughter about the antics that Kevin got up to. Thank you for sharing your story.

John Spinks, Author of Cult Escape.

Contents

Foreword

Kevin has a novel, very effective and highly visible method of relating to prisoners - he shares his life via the tattoos on his arms.

I first heard Kev's life changing testimony at a prison related conference WOW what a story of a transformed life. Little did I know then I would be working alongside Kev in the prisons around the Northwest.

I have been involved in prison ministry since 2003. As a trained tutor I oversee a course that engages and challenges men and women in prison about Restorative Justice and Victim Awareness and the impact of their own crime. I have tutored this course in five prisons in North West England. It has been great to have Kev on the team, where his passion and story has touched and changed the lives of many of the lads.

For most of the team, it is obvious from our age and appearance that we are not residents of the prison, but Kev is often mistakenly assumed to be a participant on the course. I have heard comments like, "Alright mate, not seen you around – what wing are you on?" or similar, on numerous occasions. Kev's appearance immediately gives him a high degree of 'street cred' so he never lacks opportunities to share details of his life; the lads hang on his every word.

I am sure that this book will reach many men and women, both inside and outside prison and impact their lives.

Arthur Chapman – Prison Fellowship Tutor.

Introduction

The first time I returned to prison and shared this story, the Prison Chaplain prophesied there was a book in me. Several years later, I was invited to speak at a Prison Fellowship conference and share my story. At the end, a publisher approached me and said he would help me write a book. However, I didn't act on it - not even after receiving such a clear sign. Little did I realise then something greater than I was leading me. It was some five years later after a series of other events and confirmations from people about my writing a book, I final took this great leap of faith.

Whilst writing this book, I have been met with many obstacles. It was as if life did not want me to complete it, and at one point I thought I wouldn't. I was told that my daughter, who was hospitalised, may never walk again unaided. I lost my job. I became severely ill with Covid-19. My mother-in-law (Mo) also contracted Covid and died. I had become totally bereft of motivation, but I continued to press in with what I was beginning to realise, was and is something far greater than me, myself and I. Could this book be preordained and anointed to impact and change lives? Then in the last two weeks of completing this book, my Dad, who has been a significant contributor, was rushed into hospital and ended up in the intensive care unit. Much to my grief, soon afterwards the decision was made to turn off his life-support machine. With my hand on his heart, feeling his heart's last movement, I witnessed my Dad pass away in what can only be described as very severe circumstances. I had become physically, mentally, and nearly spiritually broken. Somehow, I believe supernaturally, I have been enabled to complete this book just for you. May you enjoy, be challenged, inspired to be all you can be.

Chapter 1

The naming service

Do you remember those days at school when the teacher would call out the names on the register, and it would go as follows; Adams "Here," Bentley "Here," and then me? As those four letters in the form of a word left the teacher's lips, I would be praying that their favourite tipple was port…but no, "Cockburn!" Cue the laughter, with intermittent shouts of, "You can get cream for that!"

If I could only tell you that it ended at school, but not so. I would dread the doctors, as the tannoy seemed to explode in the waiting room "Cockburn to room 7," to a full wide-eared waiting room. Like waiting for the Second Coming, it's inevitable and everyone is going to know about it. As the pending announcement would play out in my mind, I wondered, should I pretend I have a heavy limp to ensure the on-looking waiting room knew it was my second name, not my ailment? (Cue laughter again.) Or could I wait until another name was called out after mine and then get up for that?

What continues to be a pure joy is sharing my details with the listener on the telephone. I say Coburn, but I am more often than not always asked to spell it out C.O.C.K.B.U.R.N, which spells nothing like the sound of the name I have just given. Without fail, the listener would ask me to repeat it as if I had got my own name wrong! Once was not enough humiliation. For fun, I now leave a pause after the C.O.C.K before giving them the burn. The final insult was that it took 22 years for my wife to agree to marry me and take the plunge to become Mrs. Cockburn. There is a silver lining: I am the father of 3 daughters. When they marry, that name leaves my lineage, to be uttered no more.

Let me begin my story. I arrived into the world in 1973. I was considered born sick and the spawn of lucifer. My parents were led to believe by a supposed 'holy man' that I was a baby who was hell-bound. It was clear that this was not an ordinary church baptism. This wasn't just a naming ceremony; I was stained with the evil of the world. The baptism water the bleach to disinfect my contaminated skin and purge my soul, submerged long enough to choke the evil out of me, but not too long so I would not drown. The moment my cleansed body was released and exorcised from this wet grave, it was official, I was reborn into a cult.

At school, I was never allowed to eat my meals with 'worldly' children or eat food cooked by 'worldly' people. This, together with having no access to a television at home, made it very difficult for me to relate to other children. Despite assembly containing the singing of hymns, something the cult I was being brought up in endorsed, still I was not allowed to join the throng. Every morning, I would always sit on my own, outside. As I sat, the streams of pupils entering the assembly hall would walk past and stare, curious as to why I was the only kid who had to stay outside. Right there and then, I knew I was different, the odd one out. Feelings of loneliness, fear, and anxiety became my normal: comfortably numb, hiding in plain sight.

What follows from here is an account of what I was born into and what I came out of. Despite what my family was subjected to and how that impacted me growing up, I have, forgiven them.

Chapter 2

Growing up in a cult

According to dictionary definitions, the term 'cult' can have a variety of meanings. We see the word attached to films as having a 'cult following' if the number of devotees is extensive, to give one example. To quote from Merriam Webster[1] online dictionary), 'cult' "shares an origin with 'culture' and 'cultivate', comes from the Latin *cultus*, a noun with meanings ranging from "tilling, cultivation" to "training or education" to "adoration." In English, *cult* has evolved a number of meanings following a fairly logical path. The earliest known uses of the word, recorded in the 17th century, broadly denoted "worship." From here *cult* came to refer to a specific branch of a religion or the rites and practices of that branch," more specifically "a religion regarded as unorthodox or spurious."

I was brought up in a spurious religion that twisted the Christian faith. The founder of this cult, known as the 'The Universal Leader' was, as in the cases of all cult leadership, also known as 'God's Intermediary'. The Universal Leader's ultimate role was to create the rules and ensure members STRICTLY kept to them; otherwise, they are punished severely on God's behalf.

With the worldwide Christian Church declared as perverted and anti-Christ by the Universal Leader, a doctrine of separation was decreed stating that a simple, sinless life of rightness before God could only be

1 (https://www.merriam-webster.com/dictionary/cult)

achieved by keeping all its members not only from worldly people, but from the worldliness of the Church that it had now become.

The Universal Leader's photograph was to be on display in the main room of the family home. Other rules included: I must not grow facial hair or long hair. I could only marry within the cult. Members' homes must have separate drains, (so no apartments, terraced or semi-detached houses were allowed to be lived in). Under no circumstance could I or my family visit another church in the world. We must not own or watch a television or listen to the radio. We could not listen to secular music or listen to hymns from another worldly church. We were not to attend any entertainment gatherings such as the theatre, cinema, or football match. No pet ownership was allowed (although animals could be reared for commercial use). Women were not allowed to work, (at least by the time Mum had left). Women were suppressed, subservient to, and below men. Being seen in public or the company of men without having THEIR heads covered was a sin. The only job women were entrusted with, apart from spitting out babies, was to prepare the breaking of bread ceremony, which some call Holy Communion. The job went way beyond the making of the bread and pouring out the wine: it involved intricately setting up the ceremonial table, which involved a strict rule of linen cloth-laying and arrangements. I was not allowed to be educated beyond school (16 years of age). We were not allowed to eat food cooked by worldly people or under the same roof as worldly people. We had to attend daily meetings. We weren't allowed any radio-controlled gadgets because the airwaves belong to the devil. We were not permitted to go on holiday or abroad…

I longed, even craved, to be part of what 'normal' kids were allowed to experience. School trips, concerts and parties, movie days, sports days, school fayres, playtime, having friends and sharing lunchtime and school dinners with them. It was agonising, wanting what you can't have…even if it was to simply sit and eat with these kids, sharing what you watched last night on TV. The school fayres always seemed very intriguing to me: kids would donate unwanted toys, books and magazines, and everything in between. What made me so curious was how much of the stuff these kids were giving away was off-limits to cult kids: certain TV-related magazines and annuals, and toys I had never seen before. Then unwanted music records and cassette tapes, all of which I would desperately see pass through these kids' hands. What did they sound like? The closest I would get to experiencing it would be overhearing the kids' stories. It was brutal. When I wasn't staring, I was listening intently to their tales that I couldn't share in, add to OR experience, nor did I think I ever would. It was unbearable. I was like a tightly coiled spring. It didn't help that I had learning difficulties and a speech impediment. With all of my abnormalities, teasing was inevitable and this extended way beyond school.

The aim of the cult was two-fold: 1) the less familiar you are with the world, the more it can isolate and trap you in their religious web, to keep all its members from the sum of all the world's evil parts. One grows up fearing the dread of excommunication as a punishment. Even if an inoffensive child who was not in the cult, a next-door neighbour, or an excommunicated family member dared to step foot in your home, there would be hell to pay (quite literally); and 2) become totally dependent on the institution. When I became old enough at age 16 they were to tie me in financially with a job, offer interest-free loans to set up a business or buy a house, and achieve, achieve, achieve.

The deeper into the cult one became, the harder it was to leave. From an early age, members [were] compelled to become super-religious, to try with all one's might to avoid hell and remain uncontaminated by becoming schooled in the ways of the so-called Universal Leader's 'Books of Ministry'. Teenagers would be driven to achieve holiness as religious zealots. The goal was to be preaching to the masses and as soon as possible. The more superior you became, the closer to the front of the Assembly Hall you could sit. (The front row was reserved for the super-zealots.) Then came the catch: to marry you off. Marriage became 'the trap.' The sooner they could get you to lay down family roots and have kids, compounded with the loan for the house or business, and at the very least a job, they had you tight. All this, of course, was conditional on remaining. 'The lie' was that you were free to leave whenever you wanted. You weren't being imprisoned physically; it was unseen; it was financially and mentally the worst prison of all. What's worse than the threat of being separated from your family for the rest of your life and sent to hell? Even imprisoned murderers get to see their families.

If a member broke any of the above rules, they would be 'Shut Up' and then 'Withdrawn From'. A member would usually be exposed or so guilt-ridden that they would confess. Confession of sin was often done publicly in front of the whole congregation, which usually comprised 130+ people at the local Assembly Hall. The person was then suspended from all daily services, usually for a minimum of 7 days. This involved isolation from family and friends until the local leaders believed God had forgiven them, or it could be evidenced that the person was now 'clean'. The 'Shutting-Up 7-days' rule was taken from an ancient Jewish Law relating to the treatment of lepers; a minimum of, [but not limited to], 7 days, and could be as long as the leaders felt necessary. Sometimes, this would last for many months and on occasions, indefinitely. To be 'Withdrawn From' usually followed. When a member is 'Withdrawn From', they [were] excommunicated; removed from their family home, ostracised by all family, friends, and members. Effectively, for most, this meant losing their home and job.

This is what was to happen to my Dad…but there's more backstory to be told first.

Chapter 3

Au utter ulcer of the rectum

From the day I was born, my parents would loathe taking me anywhere, if not essential. It would have to be as a last resort. As a baby, I would cry continually, and as an infant and thereafter, I would never do as I was told. I had to touch everything within reach. If it looked like a button, switch, or alarm, it was getting pressed. On one occasion, it was a school alarm, which was for accident and emergency only: a direct line to call an ambulance because the life of a child was at risk. That got pressed! This was still a time when kids were subject to corporal punishment. My hands were struck many times with a cane. Shopping was always a trial: once in a department store, I ended up amongst the crystal goblets, rolling them down one arm to the next. I may as well have been doing keeps-ups bouncing them from one foot to the other. I can't imagine the number of times my Mum would waste money buying the stuff I had broken. If Mum took her eyes off me momentarily, it would be to her deepest regret. I would go missing, found when my parents would get the loud tannoy announcement, "Can the parents of Kevin Cockburn make their way to security please."

One year, Dad was invited to preach in the Belfast arm of the cult. I was about five years old. I got to see a real Action Man, like the toys I loved so much. This was at a time when the IRA were prolific, and soldiers would stop cars travelling the roads of Northern Ireland to search for bombs. Whilst my family must have been petrified, I could not retain my excitement when this real-life Action Man stopped our car, much

to my Dad's annoyance. This was serious stuff, but all I wanted to see
was the soldier's eyes move side to side like my toy. Then I spotted the
soldier's gun. It was already a highly emotive and intense situation;
never before had we been this far from home, away from within this
very sheltered, uninformed, and un-worldly cult, but to be stopped at
gunpoint and searched for a bomb was just surreal.

Despite this, it did not stem the tide of requests made by me to get
this soldier to shoot his 'bang-bang'. I soon got on this commando's
very last nerve; he couldn't wait to usher us on. We could have had
a boot full of semtex, but with me as the foil, the search would be
eyeballs only and with great speed. The terrorists missed a trick here:
carry bombs accompanied by an uncontrollable nuisance of a child,
and they would fly through security!

A day or two after, I went missing in a Belfast shopping Centre. My
parents were beside themselves. The relief they expressed when I was
found meant that the Action Man toy I could never have, was now
available and with all the extras! Result! (Such was their guilt of losing
a child in a war-torn terrorist province!)

I was an attention seeker; more particularly, I needed supervising. Was
I learning ways in which to manipulate others so I could get what I
want? My bad behaviour had been rewarded, and to my child-like mind,
handsomely. On this same trip and a much more serious matter: we
ended up passing a beach and stopping. It was a novelty to us to see
such a sight. Holidays were a no-go to cult members. I had somehow
managed to prise my sisters' hand away from Mum's. She was only
two years of age at the time and had just begun to walk. I ended up
pushing her face down into the waves of the incoming sea. Thankfully,
Dad whipped her out without her swallowing too much salt water or
requiring resuscitation.

I didn't sleep much. I was very hyperactive. Whenever I sat, my fingers would be tapping. I constantly fidgeted. I would always have something to say, often at the most inappropriate moment. Dad could be giving a serious Biblical word to the cult's congregation, and I would be distracting him by pulling faces.

Often, we would have days out secretly as a family. We would go to Wales, Colwyn Bay, and more locally to the Wirral, Parkgate. These days out were the closest we ever came to experiencing a holiday, even if for one day only, although the day was always cut short, as we had to be back for the evening meeting. Parkgate was very special: it had an award-winning ice cream parlour and fish and chip restaurant, hence the secrecy. It was a former coastal front on the Wirral. It is now just a marshland, but still quite scenic and secluded, a place we would be less likely to bump into another cult member. I remember two very particular days out to Parkgate. To get to our destination, we had to travel along Princes Drive through Toxteth. Little did I know that one day we would live not too far from here. At the time, this was the hardest-hit area following the riots in the 80s. I recall as a kid staring out of the back window of our Green Austin Avenger, driving through this now bleak and apocalyptic landscape, witnessing burnt-out buildings and cars, wreckage everywhere. It was shocking to see. I asked Dad, "Is this what the Rapture will be like, Armageddon, the End of the World?" This was the hottest of topics the cult would love to peddle: even as a kid, you couldn't escape it.

The other instance, and the most unforgettable, was when we had to travel under the River Mersey through the Mersey Tunnel to get to the Wirral. En route, we had to pass outside Saint Georges Hall in Liverpool city centre: a magnificent building. On this occasion, many people, tens of thousands, were surrounding our car, which could barely pass through the overwhelming crowd; there was an outpouring of grief.

What had happened? It was like a human car wash as we manoeuvred the car through a sea of people, their bodies pushing up against the car. My eyes would catch the tear-filled eyes of another. It was simply disturbing, because at the time we didn't know what had happened.

It wasn't until the morning after when the newspapers revealed that John Lennon was dead! Gliding through this tunnel of pain and grief is one day I will never forget.

I was luckier than most cult-kids because of where we lived. Every Saturday, the backfield would come alive with a local football league.

The home team was Quarry Bank Old Boys. Dad and I loved catching a glimpse of these games and, depending on which pitch the 1st team played, our house was centrally placed so that we could spectate safely in comfort from my parent's bedroom window. That was until they moved to the top pitch, out of sight. Then we would have to venture outside, despite the risk of being caught by Flobbs. For a time, Flobbs was a cult leader and lived three doors down from us. (When you say his first and second name fast, it sounds like Flobbs, so this is what I called him.) We would be in plain sight if he was inspecting. But the risk of being caught added to the excitement of what we were doing. Dad had got to know some of these footballers and whilst they weren't professional or played for Liverpool Football Club, they were the closest I came in my child-like mind to stars. After the match, the team would head off to Sefton Park Cricket Club. Occasionally, my Dad would make an appearance, me in tow, which was super-risky, but very exciting. Effectively, it was a pub, a sin of sins!

Simply put, there was no entertainment for a cult kid. My Nana's Viewmaster was the closest thing I had to a TV. It was a set of binoculars in which you could insert a moveable disc of twenty or so miniature slides and view them up close and magnified through the lenses of this instrument. I would marvel at scenes from Alibaba and The Forty Thieves and the Queen's Coronation. And by the way, if you're wondering if this was another illegal sin and off-limits, you'd be quite correct.

With nothing to do, I was an absolute menace (as I suspect were most cult-kids). I would crawl into Nana's bedroom and snoop around.

Once I found her purse, which I would often visit thereafter to pilfer for the school tuck shop. I remember, when I was finally caught, how I denied ever seeing this red purse before, least of all taking money from it. If I didn't own up, the people from the naughty boy's institute from down the road were coming for me. I bit the bullet and admitted my guilt. To my relief, the imaginary telephone conversation my dad was having with the institute ended. Instead, I felt the wrath of his stiff brush punishment

Chapter 4

The allocation

The cult would meet 11 times a week, 52 days of the year, that's a whopping 572 services. Sunday would comprise of four meetings. The windowless Assembly Hall, bounded by a high wall and large security gates, was always manned when a service was on. It felt more like a fortified bank than a secret house of prayer. Inside, it was circular with a main central area where the preacher would speak. It was a 200-seater, with a car park big enough to accommodate. Many of the seats on the front row had handheld microphones like walkie-talkies, which people could speak into during the service. They would ask questions of the preacher or share thoughts of the day. There was never any music; cult-written hymns were sung acapella and never pre-arranged. One male member would often start and everyone would join in. All the men on a Sunday would have to wear white shirts and dress pants. It looked like a waiter's conference. The service would go on for about an hour, and then the adults would chat whilst the kids met up in the car park.

It was painstakingly obvious that the older I got, the worse I became. I simply did not grow out of what my parents expected I would grow out of. They desperately hoped my irrational behaviour was due to how young I was, and I would eventually grow up. They soon realised I had absolutely no filters and was way too impulsive, often inappropriate.

In my mind, I endured the monotony of life growing up in a cult by always looking on the bright side of life, or more particularly, the more humorous side of life. Anything that made me laugh I embellished, which unfortunately brought the worst out in me. Wesley Benndit was a rotund man. He would wear his trousers so high up his torso I would shout, "What waist is ya chest?" I had arranged a song I would try and sing to Mr Benndit, to Dad's embarrassment, and usually through his fingers as he would try and muffle my efforts. It was times like these that Dad was thankful I had a speech impediment.

Let me introduce you to Moses, Mo for short, AKA Molasses Mo. He was a bachelor in his 40's and still lived with his parents. He never took a wife; more accurately, one never took him. The reason he was a bachelor was obvious. He had an iron deficiency, and nothing worked properly from his waistline down apart from his backside. Often, he lit up that meeting room toilet like the incinerator at Sellafield. It was nuclear; Napalm Mo was another name! He was always on a strict diet of homebrew molasses; it was the only thing that would loosen his stools. It would not only relieve Mo's blockage, but often, it would also release a vapour like no other. It found its way into the nostrils of everyone within in its remit or who dared walk near that toilet when under full assault from Mo's bombs.

On Sunday, in between services, each family would have to entertain or be entertained. This was called 'The Allocation'. It was set up by way of a notification pushed through your door mid-week, confirming the family you were going to or the families that you were entertaining. It was quite a build-up waiting for this little slip of paper to land on your doormat. The intensity of unwrapping this note from its envelope, hoping it's not that one family you can't stand. Enter The Gormo's. This was not their second name: they were all slow blinking mouth-breathers, utterly gormless. The grandmother had severe swelling of the legs. Gormo, the dad, was super-stingy. He was tighter than two coats of paint. They would dilute the coke like cordial, and if one of the kids needed to poo, they could only go once they had received their ration of a sheet of toilet paper. Those he entertained would go home with their stomachs touching their backs and mouths drier than a Pharisees flip flop. I recall one magazine allowed for general consumption, the

National Geographic, was on show at Gormo's about the tribes of the jungle. This one was where all the women were photographed topless. In Gormo's special edited addition, all the boobs had been neatly cut out, keeping the rest of the torso intact. The last thing he wanted to do was discuss this with me, but that didn't stop me from asking him anyway.

When dinner was finished, and copious amounts of whiskey consumed, apart from at Gormo's, Dad would put on a show. He had developed his own and infamous party extravaganza, which gained him great recognition, and included made-up acts such as the laughing clown. He would sit on a chair surrounded by the visiting cult families with a hanky on his knee and pretend to laugh. He also did a Dracula act; it was simply ridiculous because he would lie prostrate on the floor as though he was in a coffin and slowly rise to his feet with his arms crossed over his chest, his teeth bucked over his bottom lip to look like fangs. Incredibly, he secretly kept a music book of all the Beatles songs, and he would sing songs such as 'Yesterday' and 'Paperback Writer'. His private audience would marvel at what they thought were his incredible songwriting abilities. To some, if not most, this would have been the first time they had heard these lyrics, as the Beatles and their music were strictly prohibited. Dad would not own up to how he knew verbatim - the words to what some would describe as evil and worldly songs. He was challenged once when a more senior brother, his nemesis, who recognised a song from the world, to which Dad replied, "It was something I overheard in the supermarket."

Let me introduce Chaz, the brother of Molasses Mo. Despite Chaz really liking a drink and being somewhat unhinged and very impulsive, he was great fun to be around. In 1981, Liverpool beat Real Madrid 1–0. Liverpool was bringing back the European Cup. Fortunately, we didn't have to travel far to witness the victory parade because we lived on the main road, but mindful however that three doors up was Flobbs abode. We still intended to watch the return of these triumphant champions without being seen. All of a sudden as the bus with the trophy and team was coming, Chaz, having had his fill of whiskey, disappeared, to seconds later emerge with the parasol from our garden furniture spinning in the air whilst hollering his Glenfiddich-fuelled chants as the team passed by. He ended up in the middle of the dual carriageway nearly under the bus and at that moment, when the open-top bus had passed, the whole of the Liverpool team knew who Chaz was. Fortunately, Flobbs must have been in purposeful lockdown because this blatant and loud act of worldly flaunting went unseen. Had he glanced out of his window the moment Chaz was making his Mary Poppins impression, he would have been Shut Up for some time.

We, of course, didn't go on holiday; it was strictly prohibited. You had to be at every meeting daily, although on occasions, you would be forgiven for missing the odd one. On this occasion, we decided we would have a day out. Chaz had hired a canal boat, and we set out on the canals around the northwest. We had hired the boat out until 9pm, but partway through the day, we learned that a special meeting had been called, as some cult members were going to be Shut Up for seven days. This was at the time of the Royal Wedding of Princess Diana and Prince Charles in 1980. It had come to light that several people had watched the wedding on public televisions or in a neighbour's house, and some of these sinners became so guilt-ridden they had openly confessed to the leaders. A special confession firing squad was formed to Shut Up the culprits publicly and allow any further confessions, so everybody had to be at the meeting. On occasions like this, it would always be a full house. So, our day out on the canal was cut short. I remember racing from where we were to where we needed to be at breakneck speed. Unbeknown to Dad I had been one to watch the Royal Wedding - in our neighbour's house, no less. Panic set in; as a kid, all manner of things crossed my mind. Had they found out about me? Should I tell my Dad first; will I have to leave my family? Despite this fear-driven imaginary theatre playing out in my mind, I was certainly not about to come clean, nor was Chaz, who had also confessed en route quietly to my Dad that he had watched it at a local pub. That settled my mind somewhat, but not as much as the relief I felt when that firing squad of a meeting was over and I had got away with it.

Chapter 5

Sent to hell

Dad by now was a figurehead within the cult. As is often the case when selfish ambition rises, others in the leadership race desiring to accelerate up the ranks will do whatever it takes, even at the expense of a friend. When a ground of these 'friends' decided to end Dad's time at the office, finding out about his flirtations with "The Beautiful Game" and his love of football was enough to bring him, and subsequently our family, down…

At home, Dad would secretly whip out a television to keep up with the latest football results and watch Match of The Day, or sneak out a radio so he could listen to the exploding Mersey beat sounds of the Beatles. Knowing visits from the leaders could occur at any moment, Dad would sit on the edge of his seat, watching television whilst waiting on the front door to knock. He would be ready to run, lift the television set and hide it before giving entry to who would be a senior cult member. As our family secretly celebrated Christmas, we had a small Christmas tree in my bedroom, hidden out of sight from anyone who would visit. Similarly, once we knew a senior leader was knocking on our door, panic would take over as we sought to smuggle the tree out of sight at great speed, whilst someone kept our visitor distracted downstairs. We could always get away with presents at Christmas, because both my brother's and my birthdays, were soon after. It didn't look too suspicious when we had an abundance of toys around Christmas time. A point worth noting, because we were soon to be sent out into abject poverty. The many Christmases thereafter were to be in stark contrast to our festivities secretly enjoyed whilst we were members of the cult.

Some of Dad's acquaintances from back in the day were naturally aware of some of his extra-curricular activities. Some who had taken part in those 'sins.' It was one of these acquaintances who, vying for Dad's position some years later, brought his past behaviour to the attention of the 'Universal Leader'. As a result, Dad was 'Shut Up' until they deemed God had forgiven him. Eventually however, Dad was 'withdrawn from' membership when matters of misappropriation of funds came to light within his bookkeeping job. Despite Dad remortgaging our home to repay the debt, together with a loyal 35 years of service, the authorities were still summoned by the senior leaders. As a result, Dad was sent to prison. Which is interesting because the cult usually went to great lengths to avoid involving outside authorities, or external influences. The cult… It bid the question, 'If this is religion; if this is God; if this is Jesus; - why would anybody want any part in it?

I was nine years old when my Dad was removed from his home and family. I recall this time in my life being very difficult to understand, but I remember it as if it was yesterday. After his time in prison, Dad never worked again. It was during one of the worst recessions in modern times. Although he did try to find work, with a criminal record to boot, this gave him no favours. One of my lasting memories was Christmas Eve of that year, 1981. Still forbidden to see his family, Dad had quietly returned to our house to see Mum. In the morning, I had woken up earlier than usual to go to the toilet. Perhaps divine incidence, for it was at that very moment our paths crossed, just as he was about to leave to return to his bedsit. Dad didn't know what to do. He was not meant to be there, nor did he want to alarm my brother or sister; plus, my Nana, who was still in the cult, was asleep in the next room. If word got back to the leaders, Mum may suffer a similar fate. Worse still, as my brother was now 'of age', the cult could effectively kidnap him! On that desolate landing, Dad just looked at me and whispered, "I love you." He pulled his finger to his lips and breathed, "Shhhhhh," then left. In a moment, he was gone again.

It soon became apparent that Mum was hatching a plan to bring Dad back home. It would be at the expense of us as a whole family leaving the cult - which to the reader may seem a good way out. However when you are institutionalised into this setup, it's the last thing you would want or could even imagine doing. My family had become so broken, was it worth forgoing to have our Dad back and the family reunited, even if hell would now be our destination? My Mum, missing Dad and struggling to bring three children up on her own, was now ready to make a decision that would change all our lives forever.

Chapter 6

My mum

The draconian conditions we were subjected to were gruesome. I know of a family whose son had been 'shut up' and was imprisoned in his bedroom for months and could not leave until he had got himself clean, or the leaders thought God had forgiven him. So much so that the other children were removed from the house to avoid contamination. When he turned 16, officially an age to be punished, he was finally excommunicated and made homeless so that the family could return…

Nana's health was declining rapidly. Her final days were spent in a nursing home and incredibly, although difficult to forget, the leaders of the cult, who simply did not like this arrangement, unofficially had her 'Shut Up' too. During that time, particularly her final days, not one of the cult members, including Nana's close and long-term friends, came to visit her on her deathbed. When she passed, the only reason they undertook Nana's funeral was that it was left in her Will, with no chance to remove the said funeral provision, (which effectively removed my Mum from any involvement). Not only did Mum lose her mother, but she was not allowed to go to Nana's funeral. We had to wait for the cult to finish burying her, so we could have our own graveside ceremony and pay our last respects. Sad but true, Dad never learnt of his mother's passing until four months after she had died, which was the intention, to stop him turning up to her funeral and contaminating the proceedings. Furthermore, and the final insult, whilst writing this book my Dad died, and some 40 years later the curse of the cult retuned yet again in an attempt to steal, destroy and shroud his final moments. My Dad wanted to be buried in his mums grave but because the cult owns the grave they would not allow Dad's remains to contaminate it. Isn't this just immoral, inhumane and utterly heart breaking? Shunned and alone separated from his family in life, now also in death.

One of my lasting memories of the cult was all the funerals and all the dead bodies. This the start of my fearful affair with death. When a member died everyone attended the service and it was always an open casket. The bodies would be displayed at the entrance as you walked in, then in the centre of the meeting hall once we were sat down. Then we had to pay our respects one last time at the end of the meeting. I got an eyeful of the same dead body 3 times so I was never going to forget these images of death, and what is seen can't be unseen. Equally as harrowing, the bodies were all prepared and embalmed in-house by a trained but not professional undertaker, who was a member of the cult, but this wasn't his main job. As it was forbidden to wear makeup, all the bodies would appear pasty white and blotchy where the rigor mortis had set in, some had blue lips. Was it only in my child like mind?

They looked like ghosts, or in the early stages of being zombified. I recall how all the bodies would smell, today I can almost sense that same disinfectant alcohol smell in my nostrils when I think about this time in my life. One of the bodies looked bloated where the undertaker had filled the person up too much. I remember one time this guy was buried in his boots and turning to my mum outwardly declaring coffin side, "Mum he's got boots like my Action Man."

A lot of the people who leave the cult go completely off the rails. I suspect the cult manipulates this to sanctimoniously claim, "I told you so, that's why we keep our people separate from the world," and use it as a form of control and fear to keep its people trapped. In reality, they are excommunicated, which cannons them into a world they do not know. They feel like aliens and are so messed up that they rebel or get lost in it, just like I did.

Let me tell you a bit about my Mum here. What inspires me most about her was that she never gave up. Nana came from a culinary background, and Mum had inherited her art and love for cooking. It was heaven-sent, particularly during such austere times. Most foods were home-cooked, some grown and hand-picked from the garden, tasty as you like, cheap, and made to last. We ate very well on a shoe-string because of Mum's culinary ingenuity, despite the circumstances. It was an amazing and anointed gift that took Mum from home cooking, to feeding the world's elite: the Queen, no less, and Paul McCartney; also Margaret Thatcher, who remarked, "It was the best salmon I have ever eaten!"

It was during this time that Mum accepted a job working in the cafe and main function rooms of Liverpool's Anglican Cathedral; "Head of," no less, preparing food for the famous, well-to-do, and dignitaries visiting Liverpool. What really filled me with great pride was that she became the main breadwinner. My little old Mum: what a woman, what resolve, and what a story! She had basically gone from nothing other than a distressed, indoctrinated, super-suppressed housewife and servant of men; to the top of her game feeding the Queen. One word: WOW! She recounts meeting the Queen, and also on another occasion, drinking copious amounts of red wine with Paul McCartney into the early hours. This was when he famously performed his Oratorio at the Cathedral. As a son of this very special Mum, I couldn't ask or pray for anything other than a long, healthy life. Thanks, Mum; I love you dearly. You stand for everything that cult was not; what I wished they were. I am eternally thankful for all you have done for me and proud of all you have achieved through the difficult circumstances you experienced. What a legacy!

Chapter 7

Escaping the cult

Getting back to that decision my Mum had to make that changed my life forever. How do you escape from a cage you cannot see? Why couldn't we see that the very thing we feared the most was everything our heart desired? We thought it was those outside of our world who were trapped! Like sheep, we couldn't see beyond our little six inches of grass. Like sheep, we were only as good as the shepherd we followed. 'The Universal leader'.

It was midnight; my Dad was making another special and secret, highly illegal visit to see my Mum. He had parked the car within a five-minute walk out of sight, followed by the usual covert short tip-toe assault on his senses, ensuring he remained out of eyeshot of our neighbour, Flobbs, Dad stole his next step under the cover of the shadows in the dark night closer to his home. He was now completely off-limits, but the draw of his wife he loved and the life he once lived was too much of a temptation to resist. As agreed, Mum had left the back door open. She awaited his arrival, clock-watching, hoping Nana would not wake up to empty her chamber-pot. This secret visit was to be their last.

What had kept my parents in the cult for so long? Despite Nana wanting to leave when my Mum was a teenager she chose to remain, in part at her late husbands request, but also for my Mum's sake as all her friends remained. My Grandad was more 'in' and my Dad was given no choice as he was still under the age of 16 and he had to get his act together and start attending every service and separate himself from the world. Subsequently, they were both now 'in' and the subjects of the Universal Leader's strict rules of separation. During this time there was a period of transition which my Dad took full advantage of to the last degree. In fact, his dad would let him listen to a radio in secret, as he knew that my Dad was struggling with the new rules and feared like some, when he turned 16 he would leave the family like his sister, Thelma who left for worldly love when she was 18 and was never seen again by my Dad until he left which was 20 years later. Dad continued to mix it with the world as did Mum, but to a lesser degree. When my parents started dating they were married off quickly. The first nail in their coffin of a once deep-rooted hope to escape. One had now become two, and so much harder to leave compared to when they were individuals. Then soon after their first son, my brother, then me and my sister. The plot, family blood was thickening, so was the spider web trapping them within this inescapable lifestyle.

That said, Dad claimed he felt the life changing power of Jesus speak to his heart, so much so that at 16 he was ready to become more 'in' than 'out', which was to his family's relief. It sounds a bit like the hokey-cokey doesn't it! Dad, a very charismatic person in life soon found that he had learnt the Bible in a way that he could now preach the word of God and deliver the gospel in a similar charismatic way to how he lived. This gained him a lot of admirers and soon he was preaching regularly, once being called to the front by the Universal Leader to preach to over 700 members. Even by his own admission Dad was an egotist and this was beginning to go to his head. Something he had loathed so much for so long he was beginning to love and now he revelled in this newfound infamy. He was a superstar locally and thought of in high regard nationally. In the 70s he became the leader of Liverpool and remained so for eight years. Despite this newfound fame he was still living a duplicitous life and mixing it with the world. Unfortunately, the attraction to escape had been further dampened by the attraction of his new position as leader, which was feeding his ego like never before.

He was now more 'in' than 'in' can be, but not necessarily because of the indoctrination, it was also about the excitement of who he had become and how people began to idolise him.

Dad had a very liberal way of running things and more often than not when the previous leadership would seek to punish sinners, Dad would often respond, "is that all, not to worry, now put the kettle on, let's have a brew." It is at this point the more stiff and conservative senior members started to take umbrage. My Dad had quite literally taken over and this did not sit well with the less charismatic senior would-be's, more particularly one man who was lining himself up to lead sooner rather than later. The one who took Dad to task over his flirtations with the world. It was at this point Dad agreed to leave the family home, and after six weeks of being 'Shut up' as a family we returned back to the meetings and all community activity, but at the expense of not seeing our Dad again, my Mum her husband indefinitely. Consequently, my parents had decided that if we as a family remained 'in' Dad could work on getting himself right 'out' and hopefully convince the leaders to agree to his return.

Whilst, my parents had never really been fully 'in', their trap was less the fear of hell and damnation, although still very real, they didn't want to lose the lifestyle they had become accustomed to. What was once an innate desire to escape had become so suppressed, they were now religiously institutionalised. Moreover, they were chin deep with a job, friends, wider family, marriage and kids; then grown up into the cult, so they knew nothing of the world enough at that point to make leaving attractive as it was before they married. Now in their mid-30s they were trapped mentally and physically, certainly financially. Set in the default position to remain, so they did, despite the circumstances or long heartfelt secret desire to leave.

Ordinarily there is always pressure to get the sinner clean so they can return and those left in the family to stay, even if the other member was not prepared to repent and get clean. For the record Dad did repent and by leaving the house was evidence of his desire to get clean. It is usually the latter that results in the family member never returning and the leaders pressuring the family to remain under the cover of, that once member chose the Devil and hell and if you were to follow you chose the same effectively dragging your kids to hell. In Dad's case, whilst several meetings did take place with the leaders in the back seat of a car outside his bedsit, Dad's nemesis was being as difficult as he could. Dad felt like he was being bullied, and after four months it was starting to wear thin. Being 'out' had started to become appealing and life had become too lonely, he had no one.

After six months of being dragged over the coals and progressing nowhere, Dad's patience had worn too thin and he couldn't take anymore. At this point it began to dawn on my parents there was little or no desire from the leader to see our family restored within the cult. We as a family needed our Dad and my Mum her husband, which made any decision to voluntarily leave easier, albeit still very agonising. On this final midnight liaison my parents met to discuss their inadvertent escape they so yearned for in their teenage years, which was unceremoniously becoming a reality, although at the time it was almost as if they were left with no alternative.

One last throw of the dice. If the cult was not prepared to reunite them as a family within it, then my parents would be forced, compelled and now threatened to reunite as a family out of it, in the evil world, almost turning the tables on the leaders, but subsequently playing into the hands of Dad's nemesis. This attempt to call the new leaders bluff unsurprisingly failed. The die was cast, we left and Dad returned home. Like any decision with such magnitude, despite being the right one, there was a period of regret. Was the correct decision made? Several years later there were some pangs of wishing they could still return, which was more a part of the brainwashing or need to unravel themselves of the same. What did bite, the very same leader who had become so belligerent in his lack of enthusiasm to see our family reunited in the cult was soon pursuing us with a passion to take my brother back. The same was absent for my parents, but this kidnapping was the glimmer of hope my parents needed so they could soon return. They agreed to release my 14-year-old brother, partly because they were still influenced by the doctrine of separation, and the leaders were not backwards in coming forwards peddling the idea that my brother needed to stay clean in order to remain in God's favour and avoid being sent to hell. How messed up is this!? I know of a family this happened to. The two older sons remained and the other two younger sons were removed with their parents. Yet another family broken up. If my brother hadn't been so messed up, losing his Dad when he was withdrawn from, or in fact a little bit older, their kidnapping would have been forever, and I would be writing this grieving his loss, knowing he was alive and quite possibly living within a short drive. Fortunately, tainted too much by the experience when Dad was removed from our home previously, my brother was not ready to embark on a life of the same, this time from his whole family. He stayed with another cult family, thankfully he was not too far away and close enough he could escape and return home. Despite several years later the leaders cornering my brother to get him back. He chose his words sparingly and told them to "@@@@ right off!!!!" We were resolved to the fact that whilst the present leader was anti Dad, returning was an impossibility.

The aching desire to return were soon replaced with the excitement of unlimited access to the very attractive brave new world we were yet to experience. We felt like the 'fish' in the epigram: "What a fish gains whilst in water, the same it loses whilst hung on the fire." My mind questioned if I could ever make up for all the good times, lovely experiences and interactions lost. But as time passed by, we were convinced: it was a GREAT ESCAPE!

Chapter 8

Rebirth

I was reborn in the summer of 1982, quite happily into the proclaimed evil world. Remember Dad's radio? It wasn't a secret anymore. I was in awe of this little one speaker box with a dial that when turned, flashed from one song to another. This airwave medicine exuding exquisite candy to my ears, was captivating. It was an unclean musical experience, contaminating me like never before… WOW! When you're used to a lifetime of "Kum ba Yah my Lord," this was like dying and waking up in heaven! I remembered thinking, "if this is evil, I don't ever want to be good!"

Dad would listen to the Top 40 pop charts every week, annotating details of the artist and song and by how many places they climbed or fell. One project in school that year was to choose an influential person in our lives and discuss. Most kids chose Elvis or John Lennon, superstars. I had no back catalogue, so I chose Simon Bates, a disc jockey. He presented the Top 40 and was like a god to Dad and me. The first time I experienced this musical awakening, Dad and I were listening to the radio, waiting for Captain Sensible to be played, learning its new position. Had it climbed higher than number 35? The top 10 came and went, and there was no sign of it. I had resigned myself to it completely dropping out of the charts. When I learned it was now No.1, I was simply ecstatic; beside myself with joy! I had chosen it, and so had many other people. Was I starting to fit in? It was at this point I unequivocally fell in love with popular music and the pop charts.

One particular day, a memorable day like no other, before or since, changed my world forever. This was the day Dad came home with a very special delivery. A box was manoeuvred with great speed and precision, smuggled through the house out of Nana's sight because she was still in the cult, up into my parents' bedroom. We were very fortunate to still be in our house as excommunicated cult members. Nana owned five bakeries and had done very well for herself financially. Through her kind-hearted generosity she bought our first home, which meant we were not tied to the cult-entrapment. Although Nana did have her own house, we eventually had to move in with her due to illness. She was a lovely lady, but with seventy-plus years of cult-conditioning, we still had to be careful.

Watching Dad peel this parcel open was a new level of excitement; you could not imagine. Plunging his hand into this treasure chest, he positioned his fingers into the back of a little white machine and pulled it out of the box into our world…my world. It was a super-modern television (albeit black and white). This was technology at its finest! In fact, the only other time I remember Dad getting this excited about something new, and the only other technological advance he embraced, was his first pair of slip-on shoes by Pierre Cardin. The excitement that rented the air was super! Now he was free from the conservative fashions of the cult, he was well and truly pushing the boat out! His new shiny grey dancing instruments were a game-changer, at least to him. He now had a shoe where he could slip his foot in and then out without bending his knee, "Look, son, no laces," he exclaimed excitedly!

Adults only wore trainers in those days for exercising, which Dad did not do, despite him having a back like an angry cat and using a wok to iron his shirts. No adults in the cult were allowed trainers as fitness and exercise were not a permitted lifestyle. These were the days and birth of the sport casuals resulting in the trainer shoe becoming the fashion item as we know it today. Liverpool fans on European awaydays would bring back names like Adidas from Germany, Diodora from

Italy, Lacoste from France. Dad opted for a pair of brand spankers all the way from Taiwan called Zephyrs. They were made of thick cut cheap suede, the type you would wear once, and the shape of your foot would remain after it had disengaged. They were deep maroon and had no laces like his slip-ons. These monstrosities had the biggest velcro strap ever seen on a shoe. I am convinced they were correctional. You didn't have to be in the same room to know he was unloading his feet from these special sprinting instruments. His velcro roar, ripping that strap apart, was such that all the birds within ear shot left the trees at once. It was like a cannon going off in the Serengeti.

Then there was the day he brought home his Delboy brown-faux-suede-lambswool knee-length winter coat. It was like something a 1970s football manager would NOT wear. But, it seemed, if it was suede and damn ugly, Dad would declare, "I'm all in." His wings had been clipped for so long in the cult; this new freedom was not doing him any favours. The coat, like the Zephyr trainers he'd acquired, were soon consigned to room 101, although he wasn't parting with his slip-ons.

Finally, the glistening white perspex box with its grey, thick glass fishbowl screen, had taken pride of place on its special little table. Dad unravelled the television wire and plugged it into the wall. We waited with bated breath for this 'pipeline of filth' to make us unclean. We were ready to be contaminated and become part of this evil generation. I had waited all my life for this moment. I was about to experience what so many other kids took for granted. This was my chance to finally relate. No longer would I have to stare, listen and wish. We only had three channels in those days BBC 1, BBC2, and ITV, with channel four on its way. Those were the days when all TV programmes closed down at midnight, followed by the National Anthem. I had watched television before; The Royal Wedding, of course. My Dad was too close to our neighbour, Tommy, and would secretly pop next door, returning some hours later absolutely sloshed on full-proof sailor's whiskey, usually with a load of meat. When the family would go on holiday, we would get the keys to the house in case of an emergency. During those two weeks, we would do a lot of spot checks! Tommy must have had a really expensive TV because we would make sure it was working every day, testing it for a good two hours. However, this was nothing compared to having our own in-house goggle-box that we could watch anytime, any day, and we were just in time for the 1982 World Cup!

It was only a matter of time before I would get to see the mighty Liverpool FC in the flesh. The timing wasn't great: the first time we could attend a match, the season had ended. However, the 28th of August was Liverpool's first home game of the new season, against West Bromwich Albion. This was an exciting day that began with Dad cranking up the "red arrow," the Vauxhall Viva. The car was the luxury version, fire red with a white interior. Unfortunately, it was 1982 and not 1972, so it was now a banger. We had an enclosed driveway that we shared with our neighbours. To access the road, the car would have to traverse this thin driveway bound by the elevations of our houses. Dad had to run the engine for about 10 minutes before leaving the garage. The build-up of exhaust smoke became quite dense. People would stop on the street as the engine roared into life, wondering where it was coming from and expecting a magnificent speeding device to fly out from this cloud of smoke. The look of disappointment when this 2-door firebird appeared! The only thing missing was Coco the Clown, pressing one of those long brass horns with a big black squeezer. It was embarrassing, but at least it was red, and it got us from A to B. On this special day, B was Anfield, my first football match watching the mighty reds. I couldn't contain my excitement.

The closer I got to this palace of pleasure, the traffic and fans began to build. No sooner had we parked the firebird than I could hear the buzz of the supporters, a steady hum which got louder the closer we got. We passed several street sellers hollering, "Get ya hat, cap, scarf, and badge." The one to avoid was the dodgy hot dog man. They had little white ovens on wheels. The man guiding it was rough, with a face like a bulldog chewing a wasp, usually with a ciggy hanging off his bottom lip. He wore a white coat, which was no longer white. I've seen cleaner mud. Those hands massaging ash-sprinkled buns hadn't seen a bar of soap all day. Ugh! We turned the corner into Anfield Road, and out from the ground rose this magnificent castle...fortress Anfield. I tightened the grip of Dad's hand; we were now being ushered along by a sea of people. To enter, you had to negotiate a narrow red steel turnstile. Watching him squeeze through it into the other side was like watching a baby being born! When in this wonderful home of football, the sound of the crowd was starting to work its way through the corridors of this concrete den, getting louder the closer I got. That last little flight of stairs would feed out into a sea of people and this green carpet-like field. Immediately, the sound hit me.

It was unbelievable. I had never seen so many people in one place or heard grown men sing so loudly, intertwined with the pre-match entertainment. The music I loved so much was ringing out louder than I had ever heard it before: 'All of My Heart' by ABC, part of the soundtrack of my life. As the kick-off approached, the noise increased; it was a full house. The teams would be read out, Bruce Grobbelaar, Kenny Dalglish, Graeme Souness, Ian Rush, and so on. The time arrived, how did I know? The Kop would start bellowing out that anthem 'You'll Never Walk Alone.' It was simply awesome. Then the roar as the players ran out! Some of the players would run out with Crown Paint-sponsored plastic and fly-away footballs, which they would hoof into the crowd. My Dad would do his utmost to catch one for me. One time he reached out too far; it skimmed his fingers, followed by him hitting the deck, which was embarrassing. From that day on, we rarely missed a game for the rest of the 80s. My first game was a win, but I had to wait until the second half to experience my first goal and that Kop roar, "He's fat, he's round, he bounces on the ground, Sammmmmyyyy Leeee," get in there, what a goal. Phil Neal then scored a penalty, and we won 2-0. What I found bizarre was watching the highlights on Match of The Day that evening, knowing that I was sitting somewhere inside this tiny TV, now simultaneously viewing the same from my parent's bed. The mind boggles!

I had close to ten years of television to catch up on. I felt like 'Johnny 6' the robot made famous by the 80s film 'Short Circuit.' This mechanical metal life form would pick up a book and read it in 60 seconds, and learn a language in a minute. I had the school summer holidays, six weeks to train myself in the art of all that is television, so I could report back to school loaded with all this information and common knowledge. The pièce-de-résistance, which gave me my first hero Simon Bates, was, of course, Top of the Pops. It was always on a Thursday at 7.00 pm, usually before Only Fools and Horses. The first song I ever saw mimed was by The Steve Miller Band 'Abracadabra'. If you can imagine how excited about the music I had become, you can appreciate Top of the Pops was just another level: especially the music videos. Michael Jackson's Billie Jean: when he danced, the pavement stones lit up. Duran Duran sang 'Rio' on a yacht in the tropics. This was the year I celebrated my first Liverpool band, The Flock of Seagulls. Boy George was a real eyeful to these untainted TV eyes. (Was it a girl or a boy?)

That massive playing field at the back of our house became a bit bigger. I now had unrestricted access, and I didn't have to worry about Flobbs spotting me mixing it with the neighbours' evil children. I met a guy called James, a year older than me. The first time I went into a non-cult house to play, James introduced me to his record player. He played Adam and the Ants, and Prince Charming, their album; a piece of art. I was amazed at experiencing this record being played by this machine with a needle. Hearing this amplified sound and music played this way, WOW. That was it, I was an Ant, and Simon Bates was no more! While I pushed hard for a record player that Christmas, my parents couldn't afford to buy one. What I did get was a Phillips tape player and recorder. That "record" button was the doorway into a whole new world. Not only was this the first Christmas we openly celebrated, but equally memorable, my first-ever owned music album: Adam Ant, 'Friend or Foe'.

That RECORD button: it was a very special button, the first-ever button with real significance in my life. The first button I could press without getting into serious trouble. A button that opened up the doorway to many hours of pleasure and the beginning of my long and passionate association with collecting music; the start of the soundtrack to my life. This little button on my new tape recorder allowed me to record whenever, wherever and whatever I was prepared to feed into that inbuilt, listening microphone. Every Thursday, Top of the Pops was on, the living room had to become like a library's library, as I pressed those two buttons to play and record simultaneously. When I held the tape recorder's mic next to the TV speaker, the recording had begun, and it had to be timed to perfection to cut out the presenter and get the start and end of the song only. This was serious business; I only had one chance to capture this song. I didn't want to hear a mouse fart, never mind my brother or Dad. They would love to let rip mid-recording. It was as if they had been holding themselves in all day for this moment, then snigger as they would try not to laugh. My face would crease up, distorted with the expression of utter rage, glued to my position, hoping that their vulgar arse trumpets could not be heard on my recording. Agonisingly I would do my best not to make any further noise, at least until the song came to an end. Then I would kick off at them, often missing the start of the next song, which would be simply catastrophic.

Getting back to my Dad, when the slip-on (shoe) was on the other foot, Dad didn't find the same funny. We had a kitchen top, which had a gap between the surface and the top of the washing machine; in short, it didn't fit. I stood by this gap and called out to him; he was watching telly upstairs and wasn't budging. I kept calling "Dad, Dad, Dad, Dad; I've got something stuck under the counter." This went on for about 10 to 15 minutes until he reluctantly separated his arse from the bed and brought himself downstairs to where I was standing, just to shut me up. He was less than happy. He had been thoroughly disturbed and wasn't in the best of moods. As he bent down to look under the counter, his head now positioned at where my arse could reach. He said, "what have you got stuck, son." "THIS!" I unloaded both barrels of my gutter gas into his nostrils. Safe to say, I was disciplined; Mr Stiff Brush made an appearance; he was not in the slightest bit amused. It was a severe telling off; a proper cult-like clip round the ear, is putting it mildly.

I remember my first cinema film; I must have been eager to watch this big-screen entertainment as I endured a musical about a ginger-haired American orphan called Annie. The 'coming soon' poster confirmed the next film showing was Tron. The film that year which undoubtedly left the biggest impression was ET, an ugly little alien with a long finger that lit up. Small things clearly amused small minds. The biggest media news event in 1982 left a lasting impression: the Falklands War. As a child, I was an extreme worrier and over-thinker. If I watched bad things on TV, they would begin to define me. I would have nightmares about being sent to war as a soldier to die. If it were a news report on a deadly illness like cancer, I would remember my throat-gurgling uncle who died from it and feared I would be next.

I couldn't wait for the new school year. I was returning as a free man, well - a boy with TV and music knowledge to boot. I couldn't wait to show off my new worldly wisdom and make real friends. Unfortunately, they remembered that I was odd, and all of a sudden, that odd kid now wanted to bang on about the very same stuff they had always known. I may as well have been talking about the conversion of carbon dioxide into oxygen; they were not interested, nor did they want to become friends. I had gone from one extreme to another: once an introvert, now an extrovert. The only chance I had to make a friend was the other odd kid. His name was Martin, and he was built like the Pillsbury dough boy with teeth like Shergar. He became my first best friend. It took until November of that year to get the official invite…I was finally going to eat food in a worldly person's house, cooked by a worldly person. Me and Shergar had burgers and chips and cloudy lemonade. I had the time of my life and was now thriving in this new and brave world, starting to feel like a normal kid.

Chapter 9

The stopover

As part of our escaping from the cult, we were ready to move up the ranks from a long day out, to a stop-over. We had a trial run on a caravan site in Wales; a long weekend. We reconnected with another of Dad's ex-cult friends. This caravan site was impressive; it had a swimming pool. It also had an arcade, disco, and pub, all these things I was yet to experience.

The most memorable holiday destinations were usually anywhere my Dad's sister Thelma lived. I am eternally grateful because, without my auntie, we would not have gone on as many holidays. Thelma was my Dad's older sister by some 15 years. Dad hadn't seen her for over 20 years. At this time, Thelma lived with Bill, her new husband. As part of the reunion, she invited us as a family to go and spend a week with them in Southend-on-Sea, which is a seaside resort in Essex. We travelled to London by train, my first experience on this high-speed locomotive, cutting through the towns and villages, watching the unspoiled countryside at 500 mph; at least that's what it felt like. It reminded me of chapters from the Famous Five books (which we were now allowed to read) when they travelled to their next summer school holiday adventure. We got off at Euston Station and drove through London in a taxi to catch the next connecting train to Southend-on-Sea. I had never seen so many cars and people! In this concrete jungle, at every corner, a new landscape would appear as if it had just grown up out of the ground. I would then hear the different dialect and a cockney taxi driver speaking like Del Boy off the telly. I was impressed.

This was the first time I had met my auntie; she was a good six feet tall. It was really amusing that Thelma's new husband, Bill, was a spit of Dangermouse's sidekick, Penfold, a cartoon mole from the '80s. Bill was about four-foot-tall, with a comb-over and fringe that started at the back of his ear. He wore thick brown bottle-bottomed glasses, which made his eyes look like piss-holes in the snow. He could never find a shirt to fit because he had arms like a four-year-old and a Ravanelli (belly) like the back of a bull. He had to wear special metal elasticated arm straps ("armlets") to pull his shirtsleeves up to meet his wrists. But despite his diminutive size, he could eat like a horse. At mealtime, he would tease the full circumference of his plate, forcing every item of food available onto his fork. This eating implement would not touch his grid until the full complement of his plate was on it. It was quite a treat to watch him pile up this fork smorgasbord, unlock his jaw, and unload this meal-on-a-stick into his gullet. It's the type of entertainment these days that would get the gold buzzer on "Britain's Got Talent." They were a double act, which was funnier: Bill was handling the organ and Thelma singing. She sang like Vera Lynn's cat, as Bill tickled those organ keys like they were burning his fingers, whilst pressing down on his special platform shoes to give him the extra drop so his size 4s could reach the organ pedals. This organ under Bill's spell was pumping out a sound like you would hear in a circus when the clowns came on. Particularly to a 10-year-old, it was woeful but unintentionally hilarious, at least to me, experiencing this sideshow for the first time under the gaze of my Dad. He was now giving me the 1000-yard stare as Mum inconspicuously pinched me from under her arm in an attempt to stop me laughing out loud. It didn't work, it was too funny, and there was nowhere to escape as this was in their living room, and we were three feet away. I laughed uncontrollably!

This was a very special time, and the first time I ever swam in the sea and developed a proper suntan. I looked like Andrew Ridley, George Michael's sidekick in "Wham". There was a funfair and a girl I was so eager to impress. The place to prove myself was going to be on a ride called the Candy Whip. We both got on it. I wanted to show her I had the minerals to go frontside, so I went shotgun in the front carriage. No one joined me; I was by myself in this chariot of fire. A person next to you acts as an extra buffer for the tight corners to bounce off and keep you fixed in place. But when this ride hit the high and tight corners, all eleven years of me would be flung from one side of the carriage to the other, and the whip felt like turning the corner was the only reason I was not thrown into the open air with a thirty-foot drop. I was petrified! Not only had the journey turned my suntanned brown knuckles white, but it turned my white underpants brown; it was embarrassing. I thought I was on the edge of death, and it went on, and on, and on, and on. The need to undress and clean myself was the reason I didn't stay around for the benefit of the said girl, who would have seen me get on tanned and come off as white as a sheet.

We got to use my auntie's car; it was a brown Ford Cortina Ghia. I had never been driven in a car that had its own onboard music system. There's something very special about listening to music in a car, especially for the first time. It's like being in the speaker, surrounded by amplified quadraphonic ear medicine. I had a very special holiday mixtape for the occasion, as my little tape recorder would follow me everywhere. Driving fast enough down Southend Promenade, windows down, sunroof open, sun shining, and choons being dropped left right and centre in this mobile dancing machine. This was another "first," another great way to hear the music I now loved. This holiday was made famous by Elton John's 'I'm still standing' and the Eurythmics 'There Must Be An Angel Playing With My Heart.' I also got my first shark-tooth necklace and a kid's onyx fake gold ring. Basically, it was a ring comprising a large black stone like a boiled sweet in the middle. Everyone had one in the 80s. Talking of fake, as always, when there's some tat that somebody wants to sell, my Dad is all ears and front of the line. The focus of his affection this time was a watch, calling him from this Aladdin's Cave on Southend Promenade, with a stereotypical Del Boy selling everything from Swedish Bengal tiger ornaments to toys that spoke in Chinese. This Essex wide boy collared Dad with this watch. It was either off the back of a wagon or made in the same place as his Zephyr trainers, which incidentally he purchased especially for this holiday. Dad was captivated all the same. He couldn't get his eyes off this bright gold watch with sparkling diamonds where the numbers should be. It was the usual pattern, worth £100, the last two comprising the one being showcased on Del Boy's wrist, and the other package in the back, ready for the new owner. This trader confirmed he had such a great day selling all the others, high demand convinced him to keep one for himself, but he was happy to let the last one go for what he paid, which was £20. Now, Dad had skin in the game; in fact, he was a hair's breadth away from parting with his readies. This Del Boy could see he had my Dad on the hook but couldn't reel him in; that was until he offered to throw in a crystal decanter set. My Dad couldn't get his £20 out of his pocket fast enough. He was convinced he had robbed the seller, talking himself up, "Ya can take the lad outa the slip-on, but ya can't take the slip-on outa the lad," nudging me with his elbow and winking, talking out the side of his mouth just in case the trader overheard him. "That's how ya do it, son. Now let's get out of here before he changes his mind." Surely alarm bells must have been ringing when the watch had already been discounted by £80, and now a crystal decanter set was included without the price going up? Safe to say, the decanter set was worth £10 and the watch even less. Seven days later, Dad couldn't get a tick, never mind a tock, out of that watch, and it turned his wrist green. The sting: he bought a decanter set he didn't need and paid twice the price.

Yet another holiday, and another first, was the chance to go away with the school to a camp in Wales called Colomendy. It was at the bottom of a famous hill called Moel Famau. This was hugely exciting because

I had never been away like this before, nor had I slept away from my family. I was beside myself, as only a year ago, this would have been unthinkable. It was a chance to spend time away with the very same school kids I could not socialise with for the last six years. On the last night, it was disco time. I had my eye on one girl: Justine, from my class. When I did my Simon Bates project, she did David Bowie, and when one of his songs, 'Let's Dance' was played, by association, I loved it because it was by her idol. Bruce Springsteen came on 'Born In The USA', so I got up to ease myself in and make some shapes. Then came the final song of the night, 'The Slowey'. I've got three minutes to make this happen. I locked onto Justine, moonwalked over to where she was surrounded by her friends, who parted like the Red Sea. As the spotlight dropped on me, I spun into a knee dive, held my hand out like a swan, and asked her to dance. Well… that's how it played out in my mind. The reality was different, but she said yes, and in no time at all, I was doing the two-step shuffle to Spandau Ballets 'True.' My eyes locked onto Justine's. I was wishing I was lucky and would get a lip sandwich. I couldn't have been happier. I was helpless, not hopeless, that I'd sure get my lip sandwich. It was a special and seminal moment; it was the final piece to my jigsaw. I felt like a normal kid for the first time with non-cult friends and a girlfriend, at least for those three minutes. I had most definitely arrived!

Little did I know my new world was about to come crashing down around me. The curse of the cult would not let me go.

Chapter 10

The end of the beginning

I thought I had arrived as an equal participant in this proclaimed evil, new and brave world, but no sooner had I landed, in the usual fashion, if there was a button to press, I pressed it. This time it was the self-destruct button.

Senior school beckoned, and I was about to bring this junior school chapter of my life to a horrible, unforgiving end. The post-cult honeymoon was well and truly over and its deep-rooted curse was starting to manifest itself. I was about to be stretched as no kid should...

The year started very differently from how it ended. It began with lots of promise, more of what I was soaking up and loving so much. My life was now seen through the screen of this little white animated Gogglebox. Channel 4 had arrived and would champion Liverpool as TV has never done before or since. This new channel was anti-establishment by being anti-BBC. It was off the back of 'Boys from The Blackstuff' and 'Scully', a wonderful tale about a scally who kept seeing Kenny Dalglish as a figment of his imagination. We now had 'One Summer' about two Liverpool lads, Billy and Icky, who escaped their social rundown housing estate to seek a new life in Wales, based on the only memorable time in their life: a school camping trip. I gravitated to this as I had just returned from my first school trip in Wales. The jewel in this Scouse crown was Brookside, about Liverpool families, which for 21 years rivalled EastEnders and Coronation Street. This was a season that put Liverpool back on the map, and I watched it happen from this little white box. In my naivety, I could almost be forgiven for thinking my city was the centre of the universe. It wasn't just the football we were championing; we were making quality music again, and all over prime-time TV.

The Tube, made famous by Jools Holland and Paula Yates, was a live spin on Top of the Pops that gave new bands a chance to be seen and heard. Enter 'Frankie Goes to Hollywood,' yet another Liverpool band, off the back of a song called 'Relax'. This was banned by the BBC and first performed on TV courtesy of The Tube. Subsequently, it shot up 67 places to number 1. This was followed by three more number 1's back to back: 'Two Tribes', 'Welcome To The Pleasuredome' and 'Power of Love.' This feat was only once achieved before by another Liverpool band, The Beatles.

Channel 4 was a breath of fresh air. The Tube was a serious music show that played live music at a time when the music and pop charts were born again. So much timeless music was released. For a season, we welcomed back Genesis and David Bowie; even John Lennon had a number 1 from the grave, ironically called 'Borrowed Time'. The Police and Dire Straits were at the height of their illustrious musical careers, and we were beginning to fall in love with U2. Synthpop was made cool by Depeche Mode and Eurythmics. The Lead Singer, Annie Lennox, looked like a man, a ginger-haired skinhead with bright red lipstick, dressed as a man in a suit. This was different, like boy George. To a wide-eyed innocent TV newbie, this was full of everything that put two fingers up at what that cult stood for.

What is seen can't be unseen, particularly when we are hurt or abused, fearful or anxious. Too often, we just put the pain in a trauma locker at the back of our minds and try to move on. Things we don't want to think about are not things we forget, and our subconscious absorbs and clings on to all manner of junk. If not dealt with, it defines you, and as in my case, becomes the lens you see all life through after that. You become like, act like, where your focus is. This time in my life ushered in a season where I was scared, anxious, and fearful of everything. What was so different about this time in my impressionable life that undoubtedly changed me forever? First off, my Dad went to prison. For the second time in a short period, I lost him. My world was fast turning dark from all that I thought looked shiny and gold in this new, very accessible world. The football I loved was being ruined by hooliganism. It was now scary to go to a match. Most fans hated LFC because they won everything. But more hatred existed between certain teams' fans, which fuelled the hooliganism, particularly the north-south divide, and more locally between Liverpool and Manchester United. I witnessed the Heysel Stadium disaster, the European Cup Final featuring Liverpool v Juventus. Thirty-nine Juventus supporters were crushed to death following a Liverpool hooligan stampede. Real-life tragedies played out on this little television, viewed from the comfort of my armchair. I had longed for access to TV land. I celebrated this little electrical window into the world I did not know. Suddenly this anticipated delight was rearing its other and ugly head in the form of unavoidable evil, revealing an unexpected sinister dark side. I was getting too much access and exposure to real-life scary events. (Can you believe that the Juventus game continued while fans were dying?!)

It was also the year the IRA heightened their reign of terror on mainland England, blowing up shops in major high streets: Harrods in London and the Brighton hotel in which Prime Minister Margaret Thatcher and her cabinet were staying. The soldier searching our car for bombs was still fresh in my mind, and I now felt more alive in my thoughts than at any time before. I was once excited and intrigued, now fearful and scared: were we about to go to war again? Then the onset of AIDS, which was so scary because there was no cure and it was deadly, more real as our neighbour lost his life to this disease. The Ethiopian famine was now raging: men, women, and kids starving to death, walking around like the living dead, covered in flies. There was nothing that scared me more than the threat of the Third World War. I had already been too up close and personal, albeit through the TV, watching the Falklands War. The threat of nuclear war seemed imminently possible and was weaving its web of hysteria into just about everything that it could. I had to ask the question: were we on the precipice of the end of the world, by way of an American or Russian nuclear strike? At eleven-years-old, this was all the more real to me… Was this nuclear threat a real sign of the end times, and was Jesus actually coming back to send us all to hell? I was mindful that the 'safety' of the cult was no longer my get out of hell card.

It wasn't enough that the 'end of days' was being pumped out through the news programmes. It was now also infecting and taking over the music I loved so much. Frankie Goes To Hollywood, 'Two Tribes', eulogised about a nuclear war ending the world. The video had lookalikes of Reagan, President of America, fighting with Gorbachev, President of Russia, in a ring surrounded by the world's press. These two superpowers metaphorically played out the final and last battle as the world watched helplessly through the lenses of its press reporters. Rocky 4 took on a similar slant: a match against Drago, an indestructible Russian boxer; yet again, America v Russia. War Games was a film about a kid playing computer games who inadvertently taps into America's war room nuclear computer and thinks he is playing an arcade game but is seconds away from setting off a real nuclear strike against Russia. This was followed by a Raymond Briggs animated film. He was most famous for The Snowman, a festive, heart-warming Christmas tale. But now, he was making films about cartoon characters dying in the fallout from a nuclear attack. Cartoon characters were losing their hair and growing boils as the radiation slowly but surely murders them, in 'Where The Wind Blows'. The pop artists I loved so much joined together as a supergroup, Band-Aid, to perform Do They Know It's Christmas, USA For Africa and We Are The World. Live Aid was the biggest live concert ever, a world concert raising awareness and money for Ethiopia in an attempt to stop the mass death of its people through starvation. As a kid, you just couldn't escape this new and terrifying world.

For close to ten years of my life, I had no regular access to TV, and in some respects, the cult's endeavours to separate me from this 'pipeline of filth' kept me in a bubble of ignorant bliss. Leaving the cult, I was the driest and largest sponge, so parched I became intoxicated with this new world elixir. It was no longer just a box of delights; I was soaking up its dark side and peddled incessantly through this thick fishbowl screen. It was subconsciously taking root in my soul, further burdening my inner being to think and act in a certain way through the lens of all that is scary and fearful. It was defining the way I processed things, and turning me into a chronic worrier. It was the start of something that would become so deep-rooted that it was unbearable and all-consuming. It was lying to my imagination, digging a mental grave so deep that I would later lie in it and drown in fear when I was locked in a prison cell 23 hours a day. The sum of all its fears meant that I thought about nothing else but death, because I had nowhere to escape in my mind.

Chapter 11

Losing my religion

On the night before my Dad was going to prison, in April of 1984, I ran into the field at the back of our home, needing a quiet place to talk to God. Even though I experienced what I had in the cult, I still didn't know any better so I religiously believed in God, it was the way I was brought up, not able to think for myself, brainwashed in to believing in a scary cult fueled god. I was screaming out loud to him at the top of my voice, "Don't take my Dad away again." The tears were flooding my eyes, crying out into the darkness of the field surrounded by nothing but emptiness. That prayer, in that field that night, was to be the last time I spoke to God until utterly broken in a prison cell some ten years later. Why did God take my Dad away for the second time? At that moment, I lost my religion. I now look back and realise that it was not God who left me, rather that day I chose that He would be absent from my life. My new lifestyle became anything goes; it was almost as if my conscience had departed. I didn't care, I was hurt, and that pain needed soothing. The world owed me, so whatever it was, if it made me feel better, even if it was funny at the expense of another, I'd do it. If I could steal it, I stole it. If it looked shiny and gold, then I wanted it. No wonder my life would spiral out of control.

The next day when I learned my Dad would not be coming home, something died in me, replaced with anger and resentment, most definitely unforgiveness. It got around the school that my Dad was in jail. On two occasions, kids from the school thought it was funny to mention this, and they were the tougher kids, the bullies. In a fit of rage, I unloaded every fibre of my anger and pain, splitting open the nose of one. Everyone in my year now knew not to mess with me. My Dad being in jail also created a misplaced reputation. This was an affluent suburban school; kids' dads just didn't go to jail. Did I thrive on it? Perhaps, but not enough for it to be okay. I needed my Dad, a father figure to take the strain, help the pain because, as a family, we were so lost. In this crowded world, I craved so much I was lonely again. I just wanted my Dad back, and it was too painful for a kid to take. Yet again, I became introverted, and the ground gained to win back these new friends and acquaintances, to shake off the odd-kid label that had taken some six years to mend, was gone. For a period, I was nitro-glycerine and just sad, no company at all. I started to feel very sorry for myself, full of self-pity. From this moment on, I was never the same, nor did I let anybody in too close, particularly from school. This was the start of many years of deep insecurity and loneliness in a very crowded place. I began to use humour as a defence mechanism, more particularly to make people feel less so I could feel better, which resulted in me having a wicked sense of humour, most certainly one which was warped. I had hoped that leaving the juniors and going into senior school would be the chance of a fresh start with new kids who had not known this messed-up odd kid from a freaky cult whose dad went to jail. Roll on senior school: I was going to Quarry Bank, the same school John Lennon went to.

Chapter 12

Prison entry

The summer of 84 was a chance to recover from a very difficult end to junior school: a time to heal and come to terms with the fact my Dad was not here anymore. When a family member goes to prison, it is not only the convict doing the sentence. Prison steals the most valuable commodity you own, 'TIME', the most precious thing in this vapour of a life, more particularly without people that matter the most. As a kid with a Dad in prison, although I knew he would come home someday, it felt too far off. I was drowning in the fact that he was gone! The Final, the most important game of my football career, arrived! I glanced over to the sidelines, his usual place of spectating. Dad was not there! I needed to be substituted off the field, and other parents tried to console me. I couldn't wait to get out of sight and cry my heart out. I was then dropped off at home by somebody else's dad. Small mercies, at least I was being spared that banger, the firebird Viva! Now, I would have done anything to be seen in it with him. In fact, I would have let Dad follow me around the school in his brown suede Huggybear coat and his maroon suede Zephyr trabs. Watching Top of The Pops, I wished he would ruin my recording with his arse trumpets again. I was wondering too if my Dad had access to a radio and the pop charts, hearing what I was at the same time. Believing he was in some distant far-away dungeon. When he wasn't breaking rocks with shackles around his ankles, or chained to a wall uncleansed, unshaven, head like a burst mattress, starving, or some top dog's bitch, was he thinking of me like I was thinking of him?

One of my saddest memories, which should have been one of our greatest, was watching Liverpool lift The European Cup together. This time it was in Rome, made famous by Bruce Grobbelaar's wobbly legs antics. I was watching it without Dad. The return of the triumphant team parading the cup in front of our house, wishing if only for a moment we were still in the cult and Chaz would fly out from nowhere with the red parasol from our garden like he did the last time we won the European Cup. Then we had been together and were not allowed openly to celebrate this victory parade. This time, we were allowed to celebrate, but Dad was gone. It was cruel; it was too much to handle. There wasn't even a chance of bumping into him secretly visiting my Mum and escaping across the landing. The same painful thought would often cross my mind when I would wake up and go to the toilet, sometimes stopping at the place our paths crossed that night, closing my eyes for a moment, imagining he was there. I missed him so much.

Dad had been relocated from HMP Walton, a Liverpool Jail, to Kirkham near Lancaster, which was a good hour's car journey up north. I was about to make the journey to see him. What would it be like; had he changed, was he okay, will I be okay? I've never been in prison before. It's a mother's heart to shield and protect her kids, and Mum did her best to keep our mind off where he was. With his move to Kirkham, Mum had reconnected with Caroline, an ex-cult member and the sister of fellow footballer mad Chaz. She had left the cult for worldly love in her early 20s. Caroline had agreed to drive us to see Dad and Mum couldn't wait to tell me. "REALLY! Yersss, double yerrsss." It was the best thing to happen to me since he was taken away. When Mum gave me the news, I ran out into the same field I hysterically escaped to on the night I knew Dad was on his way to jail. I told my new best mate, Rene, the news. He didn't believe I had a Dad, which made it more unbelievable when I told him I was going to visit him in jail.

It was a sunny day in May 1984; even the morning birds were singing louder than normal. I had a spring in my step. I was on my way to prison to see my Dad for the first time since he'd been incarcerated. The family would be reunited, even if it was only for one solitary hour. Finally, I was about to climb into the belly of this concrete iron-barred beast. It felt like the longest journey ever, the anticipation, the excitement slowing down time. One second felt like a minute; a minute felt like an hour. When we arrived, it felt like we had been driving all day, even though it took just over an hour. I was expecting a big brick fortress, but to my utter shock, it looked like Colomendy, that school trip in Wales. This was an open prison; Dad had his own key to his room. It was no prison at all! I don't know if that calmed my nerves or made me angrier. He was not confined in a cell with bars under lock and key. It seemed as though he could just walk away, get in the car and come home!

My Mum arrived at the check-in desk. "What's ya name, love, and who ya here to see?" "NOT his name, but his number." Number? What was this failed policeman talking about? In prison, you are not known by your name; you're known by a number. In fact, some 26 years later I still remember my prison number, FN3698. Despite it being a number, it was a damn sight better than being called Cockburn. I am eternally grateful for this number. Throughout my prison sentence, I was no longer associated with that burnt phallus. "Cockburn behind ya door" in jail means only one thing, and I didn't want my heterosexuality questioned, more particularly put to the test. Back to my Mum and the officer, "Do you have any sharp instruments or drugs?" Mum, so nervous I suspect, began to check her bag just in case. The look of confusion on her face: was she being arrested? Had she unknowingly become somebody's mule, or did the screw think she was Dad's moll? Was the real gangster's wife standing behind her next in line? This music-less dance around my Mum's personal security was bizarre.

We left this chamber of accusation and were led out into the prison gardens. This wasn't a prison, more like a farm it stunk the thought did cross my mind, is Molasses Mo doing time. We were guided into a community hall, the smell of the pastureland manure now overpowered by the stench of disinfectant. This room had not been modernised for some time, but it was well-decorated and clean. There was no natural light, a bit like one of the local 'Assembly Halls' from the cult. We were given a table number and sat at the one chosen for us. It was one of 20 similar round tables with a hanging light above, surrounded by over-excited waiting families. It looked like a mass gathering of psychics and mediums, and we were about to enter into a séanceathon! What did catch my eye was the shop at the back. It will come as no surprise it wasn't selling souvenirs, aniseed rock with Kirkham lettered through the centre, or a slogan mug 'HMP Kirkham wish you were here!'

After five minutes, a buzzer alerted us that a door was being opened. No sooner had the buzzer stopped than a team of men of different shapes and sizes fell out in a single file. It looked like a football team stepping out onto the pitch before a match: they all had similar clothes, jeans, and a striped shirt. "Dad, where's Dad?" I couldn't see him; they all looked the same. Then he found us! Who was this impostor standing in front of me? "Where's my Dad?" flashed across my mind. "Hi, son!" He looked different, but I recognised his voice. The Dad I remember was a whiter shade of pale, with a back on him like an angry cat, and had more chins than a Chinese phone directory. This man now standing in front of me was built more like an Adonis, a tan like Mr Bojangles and looking ten years younger. The only distinguishable feature was his comb-over. He threw the lips on Mum, "Err....that was strange, I've never seen that before." Then he threw his arms around me and kissed the top of my head. He had been on a strict diet of prison food rations, working physically as a gardener in the sun. He looked great, possibly the best I have ever seen him before or since. Seeing him like this in what was nothing like prison was very settling. I felt relieved for him and me. My hopeless flame that was extinguished on that night in the field, the last time I saw him when he came to find me, now flickered back to life. He did see Liverpool win the European Cup, and he was always following the pop charts thinking of me doing the same. What did make me laugh was his feet. AGAIN! I never thought he would wear something that would better those maroon bobby dazzlers. This time, these were prison-issue trainers. They were bright deep-sea blue with an odd white stripe arrangement that wanted to be Adidas. The whole of the toe was enveloped with thick white moulded rubber and a gum sole. They looked like bumper cars. The bumper was made to look much bigger because Dad tied the laces so aggressively, the gap above the tongue was now overlapped really tightly, which meant he had the thickest knot; so thick it could keep a ship's anchor in place, and one which Houdini would have struggled to untie. Had they been twice the length, they would have given Coco the clown's slips a run for his money! The only saving grace was that most of the other men had them on. Laugh, I did; little knowing that ten years later the same brothel-creepers would be nestling on my feet, with me the convict and Dad visiting. That's the real irony of life!

Dad and I saw each other several more times in jail, each time just as exciting as the first, but nothing compared to what was about to happen. This was the most exciting day of my life so far, better than the telly, football, all the music in the world, or Christmas Day, and leaving the cult. This particular day was when Dad got out of jail, and it was remembered uniquely because of the Olympics 1984. It was in the USA, so, effectively it was happening in the middle of the night because of the six-hour time difference. Regular TV would shut down at midnight, but the telly broadcasted the Olympics throughout the night. Telly after midnight was quite novel back then. What's the relevance? I was so excited I could not sleep, and spent the whole night watching the telly. When I was not hanging off the window ledge waiting for Dad to return, I was watching the Olympics. The contrast between that dark night on the field and this bright morning from our front window was like heaven and hell. Dad was finally coming home!

Chapter 13

Hiding in plain sight

It was great to have Dad back, but I still carried a shed load of pain. Free to make friends with the world, Rene became an important spoke in the wheel of my life. His house also backed onto the field. His best mate in school was Bumper Lee, who later became my best mate and partner in crime. Lee eventually got his name 'The Bumper' later in life when we started boozing, in his drunken state he would often find a car with a large bumper usually a Volvo. Volvos had big square bumpers and Lee could lay one out so sweetly it would leave him like a baguette and land like a king-size Mars bar across the top of the bumper. What the owner must have thought when they spotted this perfect turd on their bumper the next morning, scratching their head as to how it got there, then teasing it off with a stick. How obscene! Rene, Lee, and I, plus a few others, had the time of our lives growing up on the backfield. This field was guarded by a little hunchbacked man who hated kids. He looked like the child-catcher out of Chitty-Chitty-Bang-Bang. He couldn't run but had a little Fiat Panda, the smallest car I'd ever seen. If Quasi, the name we kids gave him, saw us anywhere near the cricket pitch, he would give chase from behind the wheel of his 'child prod.' I could move like stink, and the distance from the cricket pitch to my house compared to his mechanical Panda parked by the hut, was short enough that I could go and dance on his freshly mown cricket pitch. By the time Quasi had hobbled over to his car, bundled himself in, put the pedal to the metal and raced over, I was in the safety of my garden, laughing. We loved getting a 'legger.'

Basically, annoying someone so much that they would run after you was great. Usually, it was adults versus kids; but the adults didn't want to play, although they were forced into stopping us from doing whatever was getting on their very last nerve.

One of our favourite ways of luring in a chase would be to go apple-ing. We walked the circumference of the field, picking the apples and pears from residents' trees, returning them immediately by launching them back at their windows until one hit, hard enough so that there was an athletic enough adult that would give us what we wanted, a legger. One particular family would get our undivided attention most Sundays because their son would visit. He could run like the wind, which added to the excitement. We would egg each other on until it became a dare, and then we had to do it even though we knew this son-of-a-gun was fast. My house didn't have a back gate, just an opening, so it was our only escape route. The furious chaser did not know I lived there. The nervous excitement of knowing that this inadvertent participant was now on his way; you could hear his expletives, "You @@@@ kids, ya don't know who ya messing with, ya getting it this time," from behind his garden gate as it was unbolted! We had set the hare running. The hare was us! By the time we hit my gate, this chaser was in touching distance but not ready to run through a stranger's garden. We would hide in Mr Belmourne's garden because it was overgrown.

Mr Belmourne lived by himself, next door to Flobbs, two doors up from my house. He was a tall man but had a condition where his spine had become so bent that when he moved, it looked like he was walking through a never-ending doorway that he was too tall for. We would shout, "Duck! Oh, you already have." Apparently, his wife left him in the 1950s and went to America. Marital separation didn't really happen in those days, particularly in posh areas like this, at least with the frequency it does today, and America seemed a little far-fetched. Surely, she was dead and buried in the back garden? As kids, our imagination would run away with itself. When his wife disappeared, he spent the rest of his life living out of one room, and the rest of his house remained derelict. He lived in the back bedroom, the one we would apple, despite it being very eerie. When he peeped through the curtain, we would give him moonies, for those not in the know, we exposed our behinds.

One day, we built up the courage to take a closer look at this house of horrors. It was very unkempt and scary. Every day, Mr Belmourne would leave for a few hours, and on this particular day, he had just left. This was our chance. The back garden was overgrown in its entirety with brambles. We managed to safely negotiate a way through to get up close to the house. To our utter amazement, the back-veranda door was open, so we went inside. A pickaxe and a spade were resting up against the wall. That was odd; was this the instrument he used to kill his wife? The spade had dried mud on it. Now, we were certain she was buried in the back garden. Was this the reason it was so overgrown? This heightened our curiosity. The furniture was exactly how it was back in the 50s. The telly was an antique; it was a mahogany cabinet with a roundish screen, probably worth a bomb today. The house reeked. "Was that the body of Mrs Belmourne?" one of us uttered. "Don't be silly; she's buried in the garden." Dust everywhere; every step you made left a footprint. At this point, we were spooked. When we got as far as the kitchen, in unison, we declared, "Let's get out of here!" No sooner had we agreed than we heard the front door creaking. It was beginning to open! Mr Belmourne had returned. What do we do now? Only the kitchen door stood between this scary man and us. We were bricking it and daren't move an eyelash. The kitchen was full of empty food cans; it was like a tin pan alley. Despite how unkempt this house was, the empty tins, hundreds of them, were neatly stacked four or five high. The only space left was the space we were standing in. Any movement they would come tumbling down, and Mr Belmourne would know we were there. The stairs began creaking above us: this was our chance. Frightened, we scarpered, inadvertently knocking cans everywhere, running for our lives. In our minds, if he found us, we would end up under the brambles with his wife. No sooner had the first can hit the deck; he was alerted and watched us leave out of his bedroom window from behind the sliver of that curtain. This time, we were not stopping to reveal ourselves. In all the time we had appled him, not once had he ever complained, but was this a stretch too far.

My Mum got the shock of her life when Mr Belmourne, the man from that spooky house she had also known from her childhood and avoided until now, was now making his way up to our garden path. Ratatat, I was now in the safety of my house. Time stood still, and in the silence, I listened intently. Mum opened the front door. Then I heard, "Kevin, downstairs NOW!" The front door was still open, and I could see the shadow of a tall man. "Have you been in this man's house?!" As I looked from behind the door, keeping it between this scary wife-killer and me; as expected, it was Mr Belmourne; who else would it be? I had never seen him this close. He was raging, giving me a right telling off, his lips smacking together like a set of clackers as he couldn't get his words out fast enough. This delayed his speech. He was fuming. Splatters of saliva followed every word as he spat and pontificated all over our porch. His eyes were piercing mine as he ranted without blinking. He had white build-up around the edges of his lips which increased the more he shouted. It looked like cottage cheese, and he smelt like old potatoes. Mum was speechless. She had grown up avoiding this strange and scary man, and after 30 years, I had brought him to her door. I don't know whether she felt the telling-off was significant enough, or she was as spooked as I was, but no more was said after that. It may have been her eagerness to catch the end of Miami Vice from which she had been disturbed, as Mum had a thing for Crockett. We didn't go back, nor did we apple him again. If I'm nervous, giggling in public, I think of that pickaxe and spade: the fear grips me, and that chuckle is no more.

Senior school was a chance to start again, hoping my past didn't follow me and if it did, I made enough of a statement in my final year of juniors for it not to rear its ugly head again. For all of my teenage years, at least until 16, I didn't really connect with anyone. Unfortunately, for the most part what began in the last year of juniors followed me into the seniors. I was two different people, the kid on the back of the field having the time of my life and the introvert in school who couldn't wait to get home and back on the field to play. For the most part I lived in fear of becoming too transparent or being found out as odd again, so I withdrew and gave people less chance to comment and was another version of me. For all of my senior years I was hiding in plain sight. Safe to say I trudged through senior school in the bottom sets for everything and left with absolutely nothing. I say left, there was no chance of me returning, because I didn't show any inclination to learn, nor did I have anything resembling grades that they could grow into passes.

For the record I was never diagnosed as autistic as it wasn't recognised fully in those days. For example, apart from my inability to understand what I was being taught, I struggled with personal hygiene. I ended up with a rotten brown hole on the surface of one of my front two teeth, which everyone could see when I smiled. I was also physically a slow starter. In the third and fourth year after summer school holidays you could guarantee there would be multiple kids who left as boys and returned as men a foot taller and speaking like Barry White with a throat infection, showing off their combover moustaches. I started puberty when I was 12 and took 5 years to fully mature. I was still different to most kids, at least the ones I wanted to be known by, and for most of the seniors it felt a lot like the cult, outside looking in at a world I was not fashionable enough to be part of, good looking enough to be fancied, and too suppressed that those who knew me in school got to see another version of me.

Even though I never allowed anyone in too close, this version of me they did not want to get to know, at least they didn't think I was too odd. My seniors came and went with very little to recall but affected me deeply and only compounded further what I had gone through the first 10 years of my life, which was the root cause of all that I couldn't become or was too scared to now reveal. Yes, I was in the cult for only 10 years, but 6 years later it was still affecting how I lived. At the age of 16 I was still a boy, not allowed back into school, uneducated wondering what my next step in the world would be. I had absolutely no clue what I would do and how I would do it.

Chapter 14

Hillsborough

Saturday, 15th April, 1989, I woke with the usual nervous excitement and hope of yet another potential cup final for Liverpool. Today was FA Cup semi-final day. In those days, TV did not broadcast football like it does today unless it was a final. You either had to listen to it on the radio, watch the highlights on Match of The Day, or go to the game. Whilst I went to most home games, I didn't go to the away games unless Dad went. Up until this point, I had only been to one away game at Main Road, Manchester City's ground, to see Liverpool beat Everton 1-0 in the replay of the Milk Cup. I remember the Milk Cup final replay for two reasons. When Souness scored the winner, Dad nearly broke his ankle. He was wearing his famous slip-ons. When Dad jumped to celebrate the winning goal, he landed on the edge of the bench and hit the deck a bit like that time he did the electric boogaloo trying to capture one of those flyaway freebie footballs at Anfield. This time his ankle blew up like a blind cobbler's thumb. The second memory was the journey home. We had travelled by train. Two things of note: first, how I amused myself with the Liverpool supporter who sat opposite Dad. He had a chin like 'Desperate Dan'. The second was when a brick was thrown through the window and nearly caught him. Like me, he was a slow blinking mouth breather. When this brick traversed through the air disintegrating the window, this chin let out an almighty squawk. But what made me laugh more, up until this point, he hadn't spoken a word. He was so shaken up, now he wouldn't shut up. He also had a speech impediment to add to that ledge of the chin, and comparably the only thing I didn't have. When he spoke, it was through his nose. How I laughed! My voice wasn't that bad. At first, Dad saw the funny side. But he sat opposite this man. After 45 minutes, he didn't see the funny side anymore, and his patience had worn thin, not to mention every sudden movement or shudder of the train, he would forget he had just crippled his ankle until he put his weight on it to steady himself and the pain would leave him a little closer to unloading his wrath on me. Because I wouldn't shut up, I was getting the thousand-yard stare, and Dad had that Mr Stiff Brush look all over his face.

When I woke that Saturday morning in 1989, my brother had already left with his mates en route to Sheffield. I was envious, although I was sixteen. Thankfully, I was not yet allowed to go to away games. I remember the day distinctly. My skater friends and I had built a ramp about two feet high to jump off and over, which was stored at my house. We had moved it to the pavement at the front, and one after another, we were jumping off it trying to do a hand grab or "pull an air." Dad was listening to the game on the radio. It was 3.30 pm. I wanted to know the score. Liverpool was playing Nottingham Forest again in the same fixture played twelve months before and at the same ground, Hillsborough. The 1988 semi-final passed without serious incident, although some Liverpool fans and police officers later gave accounts of crushing within the Lepping's Lane pens. Then, the tunnel was closed, and fans were redirected to the side pens. You would have thought they would learn a lesson. In the house, Dad was nowhere to be seen. Mum explained to me that the game had been stopped. But where was Dad? He had locked himself in the downstairs toilet. What I didn't know then but I know now: he was on his knees, praying for the life of my brother who was in the Lepping's Lane Stand as this tragedy was unfolding.

Despite being a far larger club, and previous crushing incidents in 1988, Liverpool supporters were allocated the Lepping's Lane end again, the smaller end of the stadium. The terrace was divided into pens with high fences to keep the fans off the pitch and rival fans separate from each other. The game was soon to kick off, and a crowd had started to build outside the Lepping's Lane turnstiles. Progress through the turnstiles was slow, and only half the allocation of 10,000 had entered, meaning the rest had less than half an hour before kick-off to enter the ground. The game should have been delayed. The funnel-shaped nature of the area meant that the congestion was hard to escape for those at the front, so fans were starting to be crushed at the turnstiles. Then the gates were opened. Unlike 1988, the central tunnel had not been closed off to redirect the fans into the side pens. The central pens were already close to capacity, so this wave of instant pressure meant that fans already pitch-side were now being pressed up against the fences and crush barriers. People had begun losing consciousness. At 15.06, the referee stopped the game; fans were now dying.

I knew this was serious, as Grandstand and all other channels were reporting this incident live. I could see the look of worry on my parents' faces and there was a solemn atmosphere as the reports of deaths were filtering through and began to increase rapidly. My parents started to fear the worst as they had not heard from my brother. In those days, the only way to make contact would be by public telephone. As you can imagine, there would have been queues as everyone who had survived was phoning home. It had just gone 5 o'clock, and finally, the phone rang. My Dad would usually reel off the phone number to the listener "7241425." On this occasion, that ritual was forgotten: "Please be my brother," or was it the police calling to report something far worse? A deafening silence filled the room as the intensity of that heaven or hell moment increased. We were on a knife-edge. As Dad lifted the handset to his ear, time stopped. We all glared without blinking, watching Dad's face intensely. His next expression would reveal all.
My Dad declared, "He is safe;" it was my brother. Thank God! I recall when he arrived home. You could see the stretched clasped handprints in the back of his coat where people had been clinging on to him. At the inquest in 2016, it was concluded that defects at the stadium

and delays in the emergency response all contributed to the disaster. The behaviour of fans was not to blame. They found the Sheffield constabulary was in breach of their duty of care, which amounted to gross negligence, and that the 96 victims were unlawfully killed.

Chapter 15

Revisiting exams

From School, although I didn't walk away with any qualifications, I made it to college. On my first day, the principal confirmed, "We are not in a school; this is adult education. Lessons are not compulsory." I ensured I attended enough classes, even though I learned little because I got a young person's grant, which would be paid out each semester and based on attendance only. It was £500 a term. WOW! I was about to move up in the world. I had never seen this much money before. I spent most of my school life wishing I had the clobber my schoolmates had, so I was ready to kit myself out. Two other major investments were made: a Sony Walkman with Mega Bass; and a new hairdo. I was now at an age where I had broken the back of puberty and was now maturing nicely; hair everywhere, but more so on my head, which was now down to my shoulders. I was told it was going to cost £50. Why so much? I hear you say. Well, I had to have a stylist who could turn this lifeless unkempt bob of mine into a work of attractive art. The perm was going to cost £35 and the highlights £15. I gave the hairdresser the cover of the INXS Kick album featuring Michael Hutchence and said, "That's what I want". Boom, that's what I got. They did it exactly the same. I was now ready to get that hole in my front tooth fixed. Boom, I now had a set of gnashers like Dennis the Menace's dog. I didn't have to hold down my top lip when I laughed or smiled to hide the brown rotten tooth. The female students in this new college would be the benefactors. I now had new garms, a perm with highlights, but the final piece of the jigsaw was the earring. Able Cockburn had arrived! I had been transformed. I was now "representing".

I had started mixing with lads older than me. Karl was from Granby Street in the heart of Toxteth. He took me under his wing and introduced me to my first proper nightclub and casino. I went to Quadrant Park, 'The Quad'. This was the epitome of the rave scene in Liverpool. I wondered what it would be like on the drugs these new friends were taking and offering to me and which everybody else seemed to be on. I was not yet ready to climb aboard their 'Groovy Train' as The Farm once sang - another superb Liverpool band who was filling the charts with their choons. I was certainly not about to become part of the drug scene I sought to avoid so much, at least not yet.

That summer my Auntie Thelma had moved to Cornwall and was the manager of a Christian holiday home. For six weeks I spent the summer larging it in a Christian holiday home cleaning dishes and making beds. I earnt £170 for the six weeks' work, I spent all of it on a Panasonic Boombox, which had a special button, another special button, one my Dad hated as it was pressed to apply extra bass and was as loud as you like. When it was too loud Dad would shout up to my room to turn it down, I would respond, "it won't go any louder," as if he had asked me to turn it up, which wound him up even more, but I was getting too old for the stiff brush.

In Cornwall I met a girl called Becky she was a right flirt; I don't know where she got the confidence from because she looked like Thelma off Scooby Doo and had a mouth brace like Jaws in Moonraker. On her last night we danced around the un-comfortability that she wanted to throw the lips on me and I had never necked a girl before, even though I was 16, otherwise known as a tongue sandwich, it's one up from a lip sandwich. I knew what was coming, but too scared to initiate this ceremonial first. When Becky unloaded her tongue into my mouth I froze. It felt like she was licking out the leftovers from my evening meal. When we finally came up for air, I was sold, I loved it, I loved her and wanted to be her Shaggy. What magnified my emotions tenfold, this was the first time I had ever done this, but it was also her last night, so it was the only time I got to do this. At least it lasted more than that three-minute slowey with Justine dancing to Spandau Ballet six years ago. Regardless, I thought I was in love, because it hurt, and I wanted to see her again. She spent the rest of the summer working at the other hotel in the Isle of Wight and for three weeks we exchanged letters and phone calls, until soon after she stopped returning mine. I was dumped.

On my return I knew someone who had a glass collectors job in a pub called Norma Jeans. He was leaving and I asked if he could get me in as his replacement. £3.50 an hour, £20 a night with some tips, £60 a week cash in hand. What a result, I thought, but I had to work Friday and Saturday night. The money was too tempting, and I hadn't yet fallen in love with nightclubbing, so it was a no brainer. The barmaids, usually young single mums, were often eye candy and they used to flirt with me, which I loved. They knew I was very wet behind the ears; it gave them a giggle. When you're a virgin, more elderly ladies sniff your innocence from a mile away. These cougars could swallow me up in a second, that said I was too much of a prude to ever follow through on their flirtations to see if I could land myself my very own Mrs Robinson.

I remember one of the customers. I didn't realise his Mrs was a prostitute and he was her pimp. He would invite me back to his when the pub closed usually because he had sent her out on the "batter". What's That? I just pretended I knew what he meant. I never plucked up the courage to ask him, the only thing I knew it had nothing to do with fish fingers or did it. We would listen to music and have the odd drink. He introduced me to The Doors and Pink Floyd. He would always do his best to get me to have a toke on his spliff. I explained I was asthmatic and would have an attack if I smoked a ciggy, never mind illegal drugs. Which obviously wasn't altogether true, but it helped me avoid becoming part of this chemical generation I was so scared of.

One night they invited me to go into town with them, it was Halloween. It was a Tuesday night and past midnight. I thought nowhere was open. I always found it difficult to say no particularly to new things, partly due to how impressionable I was, I was certainly very naive, but also very curious to explore, which was driven by the effects of losing 10 years of my life in the cult never knowing or experiencing too many things, so new experiences I was drawn to, which heightened my need to explore more now I was 6 years free of the cult. We jumped in a cab, no sooner had we got into town it became painstakingly obvious there was no one around. This was odd, particularly as the pimp gave the taxi driver a nudge to throw a right into a dark alley. The only thing I could see was a neon pink fluorescent light above a single door we were about to go into 'The Curzon'! Straight away the relief lifted. "Phew it's a bar and it's open. This is legit after all!" Why was I so worried? Although, the same did cross my mind as we were walking down a narrow staircase into a club that had no windows and was underground. I could hear disco music and was overcome by this smell of what can only be described as oil or petrol. This vapor was rising up the staircase as we walked down. In equal measure I liked the smell as much as it made me very concerned. I couldn't turn back as I was on a single staircase trapped in a pimp-prostitute-sandwich, walking into the bowels of this one door neon lit utopia. This oil smell was getting stronger with every passing step, which was now making me tingle. The sound of this strange electronic beat pumping out from below was vibrating through the wooden staircase into the soles of my feet in time with the beat of my racing heart, which was now pulsating. Not sure if it was my nerves or the reaction to this thick petrol like aroma filling my nostrils making me dizzy. Where was I going, what was that smell and why are all the men smiling at me? In fact, where are the women!? Why was the only woman in this place the prostitute

I arrived with? Then I realised, that's why there are no women and that smell was Liquid Gold 'Rush' mixed with pheromone. I was in my first gay bar. I didn't know where to look or what to do, I had never seen other men with other men like this.

My first college academic year was coming to an end. I hadn't been to a lesson since my final March grant payment. My expectant parents were hopeful that I'd managed to do what I didn't in school: Get some grades. I had a plan to pull the wool over my parents' eyes... Back then, when you got your exam results, it was by way of a little official note with your results typed out on a headed paper slip. The actual certificate followed sometime later. By chance, I kept my last results slip from school. I wondered if I could reproduce that slip by covering up the fails with Tipp-Ex, and then photocopy the now blank slip, keeping the official examiner's headers. There was a typewriter in the library I could use to counterfeit the results... It worked an absolute treat. Mum and Dad were speechless! What a turnaround, almost miraculous! Job done, I created 5 GCSEs, C and above. Eleven years of non-compliance, one year in a college, and BOOM. They fell for it, sink line and hooker. (I would always get those words mixed up!) Despite this, I was acting in the moment, with no thought of the following September. I messed around so much in college, as with school, that I would not be allowed back. How was I going to style this out? I had the whole of the summer to come up with a plan, so my focus shifted. Another Christian hotel was beckoning. I was on my way to the Isle of Wight. Becky hadn't seen me for nearly a year. She would be getting this new version of me. I would be gone for six weeks.

I was seventeen and three-quarters and had reached my full adult height of 5'10". I hadn't filled out yet, I was as thin as a rake, there was more meat on a butcher's pencil, and I've seen fatter kneecaps on a sparrow. Despite exposing myself to my neighbours as a kid, apple-ing; it would be some stretch to do the same now, even if and when that special lady came along. I remember Bumper Lee noting my trouser leg had rolled up, exposing how thin my shin had become. So I used to wear two pairs of trousers to make my legs look bigger. I designed a special pair of calf-thickeners for the summer, as two pairs of trousers were a bit much when the heat of summer arrived. I got an old pair of jeans and rolled each leg up in a tight doughnut to the height of my calves and then cut the rest of the material out, retaining the hems and waist. They looked like suspenders as if I was a Hillbilly, and it was poontang time. I would wear another full pair of trousers over the top. To the naked eye, I now looked like I had the calves of a 100m sprinter. I borrowed my Mum's removable Velcro shoulder pads from the 80s, which I could wear underneath any top they would stick to. I was careful not to be touched in case my under-armour was exposed. I would double up my socks to thicken my ankles and double stitch the collar on my crew-neck T-shirts, so they were no longer loose.

Talking of T-shirts, I had lost all concept of God, despite now working in another Christian holiday home, this time in the Isle of Wight. To me, it was simply a hotel. INXS was still banging out the hits. They had a tune called 'The devil Inside', which was written across my brand-new T-shirt, with an image of the devil on a skateboard. This was a Christian holiday home with many holy holidaymakers. It didn't cross my mind that I was walking around with their greatest enemy blazoned across my chest. It was like turning up to an Iron Maiden concert dressed in a cardigan, sandals with white socks, and corduroys. How surely I must have offended some! This was not my intention. How on earth was I not told to change into another T shirt? They were probably praying that I would be loosed from satan's spell. They were too Christian to be offended. Becky loved that I was absolutely anarchistic. Despite my makeover and new image, I was still backwards in coming forward because I had become absolutely body-conscious, and it would take something major to get me to de-robe in front of another; nor did I want to be touched because of my under-armour. Thus, at this point, I was still a virgin. Despite my inhibitions, I couldn't wait to see Becky again. Whilst we flirted for a while, nothing happened, which in part was because another girl had caught my eye. Her name was Joanne, and she was older than me. She was also super-intelligent and went to Hull University. She was from a very wealthy area in Manchester, Wilmslow. Alex Ferguson, the Manchester United manager, was a neighbour. She was nineteen, and I was seventeen. I was certainly punching above my weight. It seemed she liked me, so I flirted with the idea of liking her enough to not resist her attention, but not too much, risking the embarrassment of getting the wrong end of the stick and being blown out by her.

For several weeks in the Isle of Wight we got to know each other but it was 'platonic' only, what does that mean? I was invited to stay at her parents' home in Wilmslow under the cover of Jo's special 'indigenous rock' like friend. We had been out bowling and returned home. We were in the living room listening to Jo's favourite album by the Housemartins 'London 0 Hull 4'. The staple music diet for any student who went to university in Hull. We dragged this out until the point of desperation, I knew what was coming but didn't have the inclination to take the lead. Jo strategically lent over to show me something on the record sleeve of this album inadvertently throwing the lips on me. Getting back to that word Platonic. The very same I heard when her mum walked in on us. In shock, Jo's mum declared, "I thought this was platonic!" The next time I had a dictionary I would find out what that word meant. Which left me bewildered because I got the spelling wrong and thought it was plutonic. You can imagine my confusion when I read it, "an indigenous rock relating to the underworld." Safe to say, all intimacy thereafter was had in the back of her mum's Mini Metro. I was certainly moving up in the world. But now excited and worried at the same time, was I about to lose my VIRGINITY???

Chapter 16

Me 1 - Hull 0

When I met my first love, it was always going to be an emotional affair. I was soon to be 18 and had never known romantic love. No sooner had we set this love train in motion than Jo had to leave to go to Germany for six weeks. She did languages at university, and this was part of her course. There is nothing more emotional and intense than a first love, which is extreme if it's a long-distance relationship. Liverpool to Hull was a three-hour journey on the National Express coach. Emotionally, I was very immature. What was this feeling? I felt more alive than I have ever been before, but I was suffocating because the very thing that had created this heart of emotion was gone. How could something so wonderful be so painful? The next six weeks we colluded and came up with a plan, when we were finally together again two would become one. I was going to lose my virginity. Then I realised, I've never done it before, nor had I been naked in front of another so panic set in.

This was not the least of my worries. The summer was over, September had arrived. My parents wanted to know which A levels I was going to do off the back of such wonderful GCSE results I didn't pass. Help! What was I going to do, I didn't have any GCSEs and the college like the school would not accept me back. I started drinking and would pilfer bottles of Southern Comfort from the glass collecting job I had returned to, and behind my bedroom door I would often drink alone sometimes to help me sleep usually for comfort. I needed a college to avoid my lie being exposed. I needed qualifications otherwise Jo would eventually leave me. I was about to make love and didn't know my arse from my elbow, what to do, how to do it. I managed to convince another college to take me on under a complete fabrication, that I had been unwell and couldn't complete my previous year. But it was miles away, a two bus 45-minute journey. I couldn't let my parents know the truth and I needed an education. The deed was sworn and for the next nine months I would spend an hour and a half travelling to and from this college on the other side of Liverpool.

Finally, Jo was back in the country and on her way to Liverpool. The loud tannoy confirmed the carriage carrying my special love cargo had arrived, so I sprinted to platform 6. I was excited because on this very evening I was going to become a man. I now knew how as I had read up and followed step by step instructions in a library book. We didn't jump into bed straight away, we set the scene first. We got a curry and a video from Blockbusters. Curry is not the most conducive food for romance. The film was called the Bear about a cub left alone, unable to feed or defend itself, when its mother was killed in a rockslide. In other words, it was about as romantic as gout. But the moment had come, we disrobed, first Jo as I moved away and pretended to look out the window. Once she was under the covers, by the light of the bear being played out through the TV it was my turn. I was ready to leave my innocence behind. Seconds away from two becoming one, Jo said "STOP!" She needed to remove the crucifix on her necklace placing it around the back of her neck and out of sight. What a mood killer, now it felt like a lifetime trying to bring this moment back to life, it would have been easier to push a marshmallow through a coin slot, so we gave up and watched the end of the bear. Well our eyes were looking at the screen. I wondered if the same thoughts crossing my mind were crossing hers. Was it my fault, am I inadequate? I was heartbroken. Was this a curse sent by the cults god? Where the cult right and had they put a spell on me? Why did she have to turn the crucifix to the back of her neck? Why was God still in the game of ruining my life?

We were in love despite the shambles of that attempt to land on the moon, we were not going to give up. After two months, eight stopovers, many attempts, it was now the 14th February, I was returning to Hull. With it being Valentine's Day, the extra pressure was unhelpful. Consequently, we both drank more than usual, enough to remove all the tension and forget all the failed attempts, more particularly the fact that sex before marriage was a sin, why did it bother me still, I had turned my back on God? In a moment on the most romantic night of the year, not a grizzly bear in sight, finally, two became one. I officially retired that boy. Never mind London 0 Hull 4, it was Me 1 Hull 0. My innocence was lost, another anti cult box well and truly ticked. What next? Unfortunately I was becoming less righteous conscience, or more particularly less sin conscience, it was almost as if I had jumped off a cliff into all that the world had on offer and this was a gateway sin to end all fear bestowed on me about sin by the cult.

Chapter 17

Jockstrap Dave

The journey to this new college was long; far away soon became habitual. For the first six months, I diligently went to all my classes, driven solely by the need to impress Jo but also by the self-imposed pressure I placed on myself to achieve, although it was still in vain. I tried my utmost to learn what I simply could not learn and so was easily distracted, which always led to me becoming mischievous. I would sit at the back of the class, bored, so I had to amuse myself.

Enter Jockstrap Dave, my first drug buddy. He had developed a sporting injury, which meant his ball-pouch needed to be cradled in a sling, but despite the advice of the doctor, he wasn't wearing his scrotal catapult as prescribed. How did I know this? I was sitting behind him in class, and it was hanging out of his bookbag. At this point, we had not engaged in any meaningful conversation. I said to him, "Jockeeeey" under my breath, out the side of my mouth. No sooner had that word left my lips Dave sat upright. He was wondering who else heard and how did I know about his scrotal sling? Dave was now giving me the 1000-yard stare out the corner of his eye. He did not dare to turn around. If he hadn't been so embarrassed and in class, he would have knocked me out right there and then. He kept schtum; he didn't want to alert the rest of the class he had issues with his pebbles, so he styled it out, hoping nobody heard and it would be forgotten. That same day, I was heading home waiting for my bus. Out strolls Jockstrap Dave. He lived within a five-minute walk of college, but via a shortcut across an open field in view of this bus stop. For the duration of that journey from the bottom of my lungs at the top of my voice, I shouted, "Jockeeeey, Jockeeeey Jockeeey, Jockeeeey, Jockeeeey." Little did I know, I was getting it the next time he saw me. Dave just continued walking. He wouldn't acknowledge me, hoping that my audience thought it was not him I was referring to, even though I would break my "Jockey" rant with "Yeah, you dressed in black, with the Herman Munster boots walking like Mr Soft." What the other people at the bus stop must have thought, I don't know, but I didn't care. I thought it was funny. I was not right in the head; my warped sense of humour would always find a way out.

The next time I saw Dave was at our Monday night Biology class. No sooner had he laid eyes on me than his head was up against mine. I had wound him up so much he didn't care anymore, and he made it clear that if my next move was the wrong one, I was getting knocked clean out. Somehow, from that day onwards, we became best of mates. Recently, my good friend Dave commented, "How on earth did we become such good friends from such an extremely unlikely start?" I didn't know, nor could I recall, how we went from a head-to-head stand-off to absolute bezzies.

The answer to that request began stirring up inside. I will share more later in this book.

Back in our early days of nightclubbing, Dave invited me to join him and some of his old school friends. We had several nights out in some of Liverpool's nightclubs, the Hippodrome and Scotts, which was a nightclub under the infamous Adelphi Hotel. These nights out do make me chuckle, looking back, as we wore blazers, chinos, ties, and dress shoes. This was soon replaced with Jeans, psychedelic tops, and longer hair. We started going to clubs like McMillian's and the Mardi Gras, which effectively were student nightclubs. We had student union cards, which meant cheap nights out. Equally important, this was a nightclub pass. It revealed unequivocally that we were 18 and nightclub ready.

Jo had gone back to uni and it became clear some months down the line that our paths were to separate. She was not going to be my wife, which six months earlier I had been so sure about. We parted ways amicably, realising we were not right for each other. In the mean-time, me and Dave had fallen head-over-heels into the world of studentship - and student girls. Jo was fast becoming a distant memory.

Chapter 18

Marijuana, Cannabis, Weed...

During my time at college, I had been around drugs constantly but refused on every occasion. Just like the Kids from Grange Hill sang, "Just say No," when Zamo was using hard drugs, I, however, was now ready to "Just Say Yes." Dave, Bri (another friend), and I had come up with a plan to make this happen. I had a contact who could get me some weed. Loaded with a load of joss sticks to put my parents off the scent of the cannabis, we were having a Saturday night in. Three lads with a fiver's weed and a blue movie. Looking back, what a strange set of circumstances. Lads smoking weed, watching a bluey together. Well, the night didn't go to plan. Dave was the first to throw a whitey, followed by me, but Bri survived. (A whitey, by the way, is when you smoke more weed than you can handle, and the colour drains from your face. The victim usually ends up being sick everywhere.)

We used to drink Dave's dad's homebrew, which was like molasses. It was really potent. There was never a time I didn't have a litre bottle of Southern Comfort at my bedside, or booze for every lad's night out. I never really got into many fights as I had the innate ability to take the mickey out of anybody, even people you dare not upset. I would leave them dry without them ever realising they were the victim of my targeted wicked sense of humour. If they did realise, they would succumb and inadvertently find it funny and laugh at themselves, or let me get away with it.

Returning to my academic year, whilst the rest of that year played out as planned and I had attended enough classes to do my exams, yet again, I failed them all. College had become less important. During this time I met Shotgun Lee, who was Dave's cousin. He was another one of my partners in crime. Shotgun Lee is not to be confused with Volvo Lee, The Bumper. The first time I met The Shotgun, Dave had got his first car, a bright orange Cortina. I thought the firebird Viva could not be beaten, but even Coco the Clown would have given this a wide berth. I wasn't really known around Daves manor so no one I knew would see me in it. We had picked him up and were heading to the beach. I had heard stories about Lee… He was proper naughty, and although he was the youngest of our crew, he was fearless. No sooner had we got to the beach than I could smell burning. I could hear crackling; I've never heard fire so loud. Plumes of thick white smoke and lots of it hovered around us. What was going on? The flames were licking the air above us and had spread as far back as I could see. What if it's a forest fire? I was panicking; we all were. I say all; we later realised that Shotgun Lee had set fire to the dry grass. We couldn't get out of that place fast enough. Thankfully, there were no reports in the local press of any major environmental disasters.

Following that event a couple of days later, the lads had gone to the Cavern, made famous of course by the Beatles. It was another student night. I met a girl called Jemimah. She was proper cute, although she had glasses like Deidre Barlow. Jemimah was a raver and went to secret raves in warehouses. She shared numerous stories of what happened and what she would get up to. My curiosity was piqued, as I had not yet entered into this beckoning new world of psychedelia and dance, but I was about to.

Chapter 19
Rave - O - Lution

It's important that I set the scene. We Brits repurposed, imagined first in Chicago from the ashes of disco, birthed on the dance floor in a club called the Warehouse. DJ Frankie Knuckles took disco back underground with a new vibe, soon dropping the 'Ware' shortened to House, and as the song proclaimed, "Jack boldly declared, Let there be House, and House music was born." Frankie Knuckles was soon sworn in as 'The Godfather of House,' and this was the first time DJs started to control the crowd. It wasn't just about playing records anymore; it was about mixing the right tracks. In doing so, Knuckles took disco music and changed it into something new. He brought the energy of the gay and black dance scenes from the underground, back into the clubs and dance floors of Chicago. It was the type of music that would grab the soul. DJs began digging their vinyl crates, bringing back to life old disco songs, but speeding them up and mixing them. In the mix, six minutes could be shortened, cutting out the filler, playing only the meat of the songs, the best parts. It was all about one record going with another, usually the beat of one song with the disco vocals of the other. Three years after the Chicago House was established, its position as the next new thing crossed the Atlantic to England. Little did its creators know, no sooner had this new rave wave landed, than it was winning over dance floors from Liverpool to Ibiza. The energy of these clubs made these high-octane nights exhilarating. The drugs compelling ravers to party way beyond the 2.00 a.m. club closedown.

Such demand birthed the move into illegal warehouse after-hour parties, which then went outdoors into farmers' fields. Parties arranged by invite-only, from a random telephone box. The special message would send you to a service station, and the convoy would head out to the illegal party. The big illegal rave anthem was 'Everything starts with an E' by the Easy Posse.' The lyrics started the demon drug narrative, sensationalism across the headlines of the newspapers claiming such music was inciting the kids and the youth to consume drugs. Consequently, Radio 1 banned it, which fuelled interest and in response, Acid House took over the nation. That was until the gangster element ruined it. The police finally stepped up the pressure, and the government entered the frame, making these parties highly illegal. The press did eulogise at one point and called this scene cool; some printed a guide to the slang and even ran a special offer for smiley T-shirts. This was soon replaced by the evil of club drugs that cause heart attacks and brain damage. The drugs were cut with rat poison, heroin, and embalming fluid. The effects would last for up to twelve hours, with panic attacks and flashbacks and the probability of being sexually assaulted under the influence. "Acid House Horror" was the headline prompting other similar headlines like 'A Trip to an Evil Night of Ecstasy'. As the newspapers engaged in a contest to see who could come up with the most distorted headlines, some reported outrageous sex was taking place on special stages in front of the dance floor. It was claimed the screaming teenagers were like demented demonic dolls, as the drugs they swallowed an hour earlier took their terrible toll. They had become possessed, sucked into a hellish nightmare.

Club promoters started hiring out warehouses and took over big stage nightclubs. One example near me was The Quadrant Park in Liverpool, was the first nightclub to do an all-nighter. In the summer of 1989, House music was on the top of the Charts with 'Ride On Time' by Black Box; but at a time that signalled the end of the first rave wave. That was until 1991, with the help of the Hacienda and the Madchester scene. The Stone Roses, 808 State, and the Happy Mondays brought a song out called 'Wrote For Luck', remixed by Paul Oakenfold. This was the coming together of dance and rock music. The video is best remembered by Shaun Ryder appearing to be off his head on 'E', contorting in the middle of the Hacienda dance floor. As we entered the 90s, the charts were now taken over completely by this second rave wave. In the last months of 1991, most of the Top 40 songs were dance and rave songs comprising a series of anthems covering the full spectrum on offer such as Moby 'Go', Prodigy 'Everybody in the Place,' Alternate 'Evapor8', Bassheads 'Is there Anybody out There,' K-Class 'Show me Love,' SL2 'On a Ragga Trip,' N-Joi 'Anthem,' and 2 Unlimited 'Get Ready for This'. We were 'Ready For This,' three nomadic friends for life: Dave, The Bumper, and me. It was our time, like the Flower Power Hippies, Disco Freaks, and Northern Soulers. We were on the cusp, entering the next generational movement. The promise of this new uplifting and exciting House dance rave scene was beckoning, and we were oblivious to the fact we were about to be grown up into a pursuit of self-discovery and a higher state of consciousness. One last chance to celebrate our disappearing youth, borne out of an innate need, which is in all of us, to become someone. At the very least, become part of something, a union of like-minded people, a desire to be fulfilled, a religion, a cult even, or more pertinently, a Rave-o-lution. This was the time I witnessed; my generation standing on the shoulders of those scenes that have gone before. It was the next generational movement Frankie Knuckles so ceremonially gave rise to, and the development of electronic dance music, namely House music and its electronic offspring, 'Rave'. I believed I was in the right place at the right time.

Chapter 20

God is a DJ?

For close to seventeen years, I was teetotal. In fact, I was afraid of cigarettes. From fourteen years of age, most kids I knew spent most of the weekend on a field, drunk; some getting their stomachs pumped, smoking like chimneys, and soon, indulging in cannabis. Whilst I had found comfort in alcohol, I was 18, and a year later, I endured a misplaced session smoking cannabis which made me sick. Looking back, it makes me wonder why I was so drawn to this rave movement and drug culture, but as I unpack my story it perhaps does explain why - and why so many others are, too. Being part of something anti-establishment, a youth movement, of which taking illegal drugs was a big part, created the thrill that fuelled this new scene. But I wasn't a thrill-seeker. Was I in pursuit of self-discovery, catching up on all those years lost in the cult? Did I really crave rediscovery? Did I have a need to be found and fulfilled? Was I actually lost? Did I need a revelation of the world that grew me up to make sense of the one I was now living in? Did I need to escape? If so, what was I escaping to and from? Had the life I lived become comfortably numb so that I did not have to think too hard and long about my past? How on earth did I become a heavy drug user and abuser? It still shocks me when wonder how I left the cult a complete puritan that within 10 years I would go from one extreme to another. From the cult to jail.

Nine years after I left the cult, surely it didn't matter anymore? Was it too late? Had something taken root? Did I have issues I had not dealt with? Life after that, was spent trying to grow up and out of my past. I certainly didn't want to think about the future, adulthood, or dwelling on the fragility of life. Why was I so preoccupied with death? Why was I so damn stressed? I certainly was comforted by Southern Comfort, and I was always drunk before anyone else when we went out. Was I starting to join up the dots? Drinking behind my bedroom door was the start of comfort-seeking and all manner of substance abuse. So much so that after eighteen years of living clean, within two short years thereafter I would use and abuse almost anything and everything of a chemical nature. I can't think of any other explanation other than I was a messed-up kid that hid in plain sight, old enough to hide in substance abuse instead. Am I digging too deep? Will I ever make sense of the cards I was dealt? Is it any wonder illegal chemicals would give me a release from my morbid, worrisome, sometimes stark sense of reality and mortality? If I could go back in time and ask that nineteen-year-old version of me two questions, it would be these: "Why was I obsessed with the idea that I was going to die soon"? "Did I really believe the cult had sent me to hell?"

The answer to why I (and therefore others) turned to a life of drugs, was that taking substances made me feel loved. My dry soul filled with a drug-induced sense of spirituality gave a feeling of self-worth, love for others - the opposite to what the cult displayed and anything else I felt thereafter. When I experienced an illegal high, at that moment, I could breathe… It felt like that for the first time, and every time after that, so I was ready to do whatever it took with no thought of the future or my past. I decided ahead of my cult-sentenced appointment with hell that I was going to get busy living; at the very least busy *myself* with living, so I did not have to think too hard about my life that drug use and abuse would soon expose: The drug high opened up my hurt locker of normalised pain from the past, which made the synthetic highs infinitely more euphoric. Unfortunately, the comedown was so much deeper, which led to the need to self-soothe with drugs daily. After drug use, the pain of the past no longer felt normal. I needed to escape from it by regularly smoking weed, living for the weekend and experiencing Ecstasy. But it was a false economy, as in a temporary state of release from the asylum. The insanity, hidden for too long in the back of my mind, was blown into oblivion for one night only, giving way to a drug-induced feeling of self-therapy, arrival and fulfilment, at least until the drugs wore off.

Despite my time in the cult, I never really worshipped anything, then or since, not even myself. Hate is a strong word. I certainly disliked who I was, which was driven through the lens of all my deep insecurities borne out of the first ten years of my life. Since then, I have not been part of anything, never mind something, at least by choice. In the cult, I had no choice. This created a bed of resentment and unforgiveness, which fuelled the drip-fed pain that had woven itself, slowly, surely, and secretly into every fibre of my being. So, of course, I needed a release from the pain. What if it's in another realm of pure unadulterated hedonistic pleasure? My life was starved of meaning and purpose for far too long. I lacked a higher opinion of self-worth; I needed something greater to strive towards. This is what my soul always craved and could not be satisfied whether it be in the cult, or any religious establishment my parents would drag me along to. Even then, I knew authentic worship was about spiritually lifting that individual from within their soul and heart, so they would walk in one way and leave by another. I did walk in one way; I would always leave much worse. Maybe it was because 'the message' just wasn't communicated in a way that met me where I was at. Maybe it was because I carried so much fear, I didn't want to be around religious people. Maybe I simply hadn't forgiven the cult peddled God who destroyed my family and ruined my life for 10 years, arguably the most important years of my life. All I knew was I wanted to get out of these places as quick as possible.

THAT was until the next season in my life. I was about to be taken back to a 'church', one like no other I had experienced before. This was a different place of worship. The Godfather of House music, Frankie

Knuckles, once sermonised that clubs are like churches; by the time the preacher gets going, the whole room becomes one.

"Sometimes I feel like throwing my hands up in the air, Lord, you've got the love I need to see me through….When the angels from above fall down and spread their wings like doves and we'll walk hand in hand, sisters, brothers, we'll make it to the Promised Land…….. I've got peace deep in my soul, I've got love making me whole since you opened up your heart and shined on me." These some of the lyrics to the new hymn book of my life, the same I danced the night away to. A song by Faithless that put my life back then into perspective. "This is my church; this is where I heal my hurts. It's in natural grace, solutions and remedies, enemies becoming friends when bitterness ends, God is a DJ." Just as the devout have their places of worship, raving provided at least for me, the same physical outlet as a partier for the frustration, delight and perplexity that accumulates from the trials and tribulations of my everyday life. But unfortunately this was no an edifying experience because I was enjoying these gospel dance songs under the influence of drugs.

The deception, I thought I had found something; like salvation, but through drugs and dance music. Why would'nt I? I saw the dance floor dissipate class, ethnicity, gender, and other social distinctions. We loved dancing under one roof to the same beat, trailblazing a path to the promised land, the mass movement or a rave nation, a brotherhood. Was the nightclub changing the role that organised religion, the church, failed to do, lifting us onto the sacramental and supramental plane? A traditional hymn once declared, "Onward Christian Soldiers, Marching as to War." Were the same people still marching, but now to the beat of Ecstasy, which conjures up an image of innocent youth seduced by a pharmacological pied piper? More particularly, the counterfeit Trinity: god the DJ, god the dealer, and Ecstasy the unholy spirit. It didn't feel dark and sinister at the time; in fact, it felt euphoric and heavenly. Instead of the Ministry of the Bible, we had the Ministry of

Sound. Looking back, it makes me think that it was the devil copying the greatest movement ever: the day of Pentecost, the day the Church began, when the Holy Spirit fell like a Dove and 3000 people danced and praised the Lord. Interestingly, 2000 years later we were doing the same on Ecstatsy and the most common tablet was named a Dove. Was it a counterfeit experience sent from hell, now re-presented masquerading as the same, a drug-induced spirituality, parading as superficial love and peace but subliminally driving the unsuspecting users down a tunnel destined for a chemical-induced depression - a kind of prolonged youth suicide.

Thirty years on, what has happened to my generation, I am not sure how we will be remembered and what we will be remembered for, but it will not be a legacy of great value, at least compared to those that we grew up from. Think about it, my parents and their parents' parents who went through two world wars. Liverpool, one of the most bombed cities in England. People were living in real fear daily of whether they would see out the day or wake up alive, surviving on rationed foods, nearly to a man and woman these wonderful shouldered people we stand on did not become a Prozac generation and compared to our generation it would have been understandable and forgivable. Our generation who have for the most part never been in a war zone, in fact many have had access to all their heart desired, more medical advances and greater life expectancy, including a quality of life unlike never before, yet so many of us are unhappy, unsatisfied and discontent. More saddening, depression and suicide is one of the biggest killers in our age, particularly in young men it's up there with abortion. Can you see a theme, can you see the problem, we don't need a war or a pandemic to control the population, society has been so brainwashed and messed up HUMANS ARE KILLING HUMANS WITHOUT THE NEED FOR WAR! HELP!

Back then, in the cold light of day or under the warm dance floor of the night, I didn't care about the consequences, and I was ready to push all my chips into the centre of this self-discovery, hedonistic table. I was ready to soak up and in, that thick and sticky attitude of sensuality. This was my new religion, and I, the god of my universe, based on my feelings experienced on the dance floor and drugs. This scene released me from the pain drain, enough that I wanted to do it again and again. I was sure if it made me feel good, it must be right, and anything goes, so I will do what I want, how I want, and with whomever I want.

Chapter 21

The Berghaus ninja

A club called the Academy would widen my nocturnal activities to new pastures, despite the admission being twice the price of my usual haunts. Off the bat, this was different; outside there was a buzz I had not experienced before. This place could hold up to 2,000 people. Queuing with these acid house nomads at this new club added to the excitement. We were used to a basement, which was dark and dingy with disco lights, 500 people at the most. In fact, we never had to queue. Interestingly, the very same club I was about to enter would later be renamed and become the biggest club in Europe, not in size, but in credibility. Alarmingly, this nightclub would become my future place of work from which I would sell Class A drugs; and the place of my arrest. We paid our £10 entry fee and made our way through security, passing the cloakroom hatch. It was summer, so we had nothing to declare. The reception looked like a womb, not only in the visceral sense, but it looked like something which the entrance doors ahead were about to birth us out of and into. The thumping bass had notched up the excitement as we queued; we were now in this birth canal. The echo of the deep bass beat had crystallised from a dark melodic thud to something that made me want to dance right there and then. Once beyond the doors, effectively born again and out of this makeshift womb, the electronic bass being played out across this Warehouse was louder than I have ever heard before. You could feel the music before you heard it. It was hypnotic and alluring. I began to wonder what it would be like, high on drugs, like 'Everybody In The Place' already was, the name of a famous rave tune from back in the day.

A once-dreary black building had been fantasised with all manner of fairy tale adaptation into a psychedelic wonderland. It was like stepping into Willy Wonka's secret chocolate factory imagined on "ACIEEEED". The walls were covered with projector screens playing scenes of armies marching backwards and pixies dancing upside down, psychedelic swirls, curls, and everything in between. Every time the DJ dropped a big phat bassline, the strobe would kick in. As the pumping oscillating piano solo pumped out, the bubble machine would incessantly spit out its weightless teardrops. Bubbles of all sizes and shapes would fall like acid rain across this dance floor, saturating the hedonistic druggies, this their only chance of respite; as their drug-fuelled bodies overheated, the bubble disintegrating on the sweaty ravers' skin. The rhythmic, repetitive beat, now under the spell of the smoke, filled bright neon teal lasers like a conductor would control an orchestra. The dancers would intersect as they raised their hands, some stripped to the waist, sweating, bobbing and weaving, as if practising some ritual secret tribal dance or martial art, etching strange signs in the air, some with white gloves, high-vis vests, horns, whistles and face masks filled with Vicks vapour rub, mixed up with the smell of Liquid Gold (rush), freshening the air. As the diva screamed out her uplifting vocals, she was accompanied by a piano crescendo, raising the anticipation as the participants nomadically sought to recreate heaven on earth. Then, at a preordained moment, with only synthesized electronic piano pumping out of the speakers, the lights would go up, and everybody's hands were now in the air, stretching out to the heavens as if it was in touching distance, some with palms open, expecting to receive an impartation.

Was this a nightclub or a church, or both? I felt like I had been reformed; it felt spiritual. Everyone on the dance floor worshipped the DJ as the exhilarating underground music pumped out of the super-sized speakers. It was time to dance. I was ready to give it a go. I learned new dance moves in a moment; they would spread throughout the crowd like a superfast virus. The rave wave with me now instantly participating trained me in a new kind of dancing, agitating my body with twitches, jerks, spasms, and ticks. This was dancing anybody could do, a unity of free self-expression fused in a force field of reverberating piano riffs and pulsating bass drops. The crowd was being evangelised from the 'pulpit', the DJ's box, and us, the 'congregation'. When we weren't reaching for the heavens, we would use our hands to create the shape of a 'T' for Tune, to acknowledge this was an absolutely bangin' CHOOOON! The excitement of leaving one track and hearing the next track slowly but surely being mixed in! This was not about the bands or even the name of the songs, it was all about a 12-inch circle of wax, with the DJ as the focal point and the flow of the mix, their 'ministry'. I was a believer. I had turned up, tuned in, and freaked the hell out. We landed in the chill-out area. Bean bags were laid out in front of a cinema screen playing Snow White and Seven Dwarfs. Dave, The Bumper, and I sat in momentary silence soaking in the atmosphere, almost in disbelief. Yes, we had run out of steam. However, what was obvious was that this was not a night best enjoyed inebriated. If we wanted to experience this scene in full living breathing technicolour, we had to be high. As one song declared: "Gonna Touch the Sky, Never Been This High." What did that feel like?

Despite failed attempts to get qualifications at the 'bus journey' college, I had evidenced by attendance that I was worthy of a second chance. I was still driven, of course, at least by the need to be seen to be learning by my parents, albeit there was no need for a tale this time. With every new academic year came new friends. I was invited to attend an event with several new college acquaintances, where they 'worshipped' most Monday nights. Straight off the bat, this sounded different. It was Monday night, for starters, absolutely no one goes out on this night, and even the chip shop's closed. I would be picked up around 7.30. The only instructions were, "wear something casual," the brighter, the better. The night would be alcohol-free; not even holy communion was on offer. I wanted to experience this promise of a spiritual evening like these new friends told me they had experienced many times, so it was a prerequisite for me to remain sober. "Mum, Dad, I'm going out, and I am not sure what time I will be back," I excitedly proclaimed. "What, on a Monday night?" "Yeah." This was unusual, so Dad quizzed me further, "With Lee and Dave?" "No!" This heightened my Dad's curiosity. Why was I on my way out on a Monday evening, and who were these new friends picking me up? For several weeks in the café of the college, I heard stories about nights of spiritual euphoria. Would I be in a sea of 1,000 radiant souls, putting into practice five thousand years of worshipping? A tribal gathering experiencing spirituality put in place by our ancestors, now available to the youth culture of the day? My new friends where sure on that night I was about to have an experience that would change my life forever.

Safely tucked away in the back of a Ford Escort Ghia, I was about to do something I've never done before. I was going to a place I had never been to before called Aintree. Although I had known it from the Grand National, that was all I knew. I remember marvelling in the darkness at the sheer size of this racecourse as I spotted it sprawling across my peripheral vision out of this Escort window. Still, we were going in the other direction and soon turned off the main road. The lane was now single file, and we passed under a bridge into an area of light industrial buildings. I knew we were getting close to our destination as the traffic increased, and there were lots of foot passengers; swarms of lads all dressed in outdoor gear, even though we were going indoors. Berghaus was the name on the coat. I became nervous because this was the staple uniform of 'The Scall' (Scally).

Let me introduce Dezzy 'The Bear', He was a scall. He lived around the corner from my family home, but he was a next level nut Job. When he was eight years of age, he was knocking out teenagers and every kid that lived in my neighbourhood was petrified of him. If you saw him anywhere you would turn and go the other way. I remeber seeing him glass a man in a pub. Usually he would knock anyone out who dare step in his path, but he never touched me, not even for fun. In fact, he thought he was my friend and I had to be his, which in fairness I had no choice and I was too scared to say no.

A couple of years went by and I heard many stories confirming what Dezzy was now getting up to. It wasn't good. I was now 18 he would have been 15, but he was a unit and looked like a young adult. This car pulled up next to me on my way to college. It was Dezzy. Whilst I did my best to avoid his kind offer of a lift, I knew it was a robbed car and he was too young to drive. In that moment I was treading a very fine line bricking it between getting in a stolen car with him and saying no when he was so insistent. I chose the easy option as the last thing I wanted to do was become his adversary, which if you said no usually followed. I climbed in, it felt like the easy option, although it took me back to that fair ride in Southend 'The Candy Whip' unfortunately this time there was no girl to impress and I had followed through before riding. I was in this car under duress, a joy rider, straight away I noticed he had about 30 stitches in his hand. He saw that I saw, so he had to tell me he got them when he smashed open the window of the last car he robbed. Whilst that Journey lasted five minutes it felt like five hours. I was not sure which frightened me the most, the Police catching me in this car, kids were getting 6 months in Juveniles centres. Plus, this was a time kids robbing cars were being paralysed, killed or worse decapitated, which happened for real several weeks prior to this similar journey I was now slap bang in the middle of. That car was totalled and all four Scall's were killed instantly. Usually, like Dezzy, these kids could not drive properly and it was all about the speed, and often Police cars would chase them into walls, lamp posts and trees, the aim was to get them off the road, better the joy riders dead, than the innocent public

The Bear who thought speed was spelt STOP and GIVE WAY meant make a hand break turn was in full flight, so I could not stop my mind racing as fast as this car, pertrified. This was one of the scariest situations I had been in. Whilst I managed to get to my destination without the threat of having to duck under the shattered guillotine like shards of windscreen or leaving behind a limb, all manner of major car tragedy, and death was being played out in the theatre of my mind. As soon as I got out of that car and walked through the college gates out of sight of Dezzy, I ran to the nearest toilet. Before cleaning out my underwear, I sat on on that throne of safety out of sight, I was so spent and started comfort rubbing my other arm, whilst rocking back and forth, my bottom lip was going like the clappers, chanting under my breath "I don't want to die and don't want to die." I later learnt when Dezzy turned 21 soon after he was found dead from a heroin overdose, an addiction he developed when he was sent to jail for 5 years for rape.

Quite simply a Scall was not psychedelic rave hippy like the ones I met in in the Academy. In fact because of The Bear I would go to great lengths to avoid these characters. Local Wiki described 'The Scall' as follows.

"To call someone a scally is to presume they are either one or all of the following: poorly housed and prejudiced for example racist, misogynist, homophobic, ill-educated, unemployed in possession of either a criminal record or criminal intent of uncertain lineage. A typical Liverpool scally is easy to identify by their clothing. They often wear dark tracksuits (often tucked into their socks) and a hooded coat or top to help disguise their face. This dress code has led to them being referred to as "ninjas" by some people. It is also common to see male scallies putting their hands down the front of their trousers. Nobody seems to know why they do this, although it could be some kind of autoerotic act or simply to hold on to their penises to prevent them from disappearing. They also often talk in a "thick" scouse accent which is exaggerated for effect."

Not my words! Assuming this was a fair description, this was the very same indigenous native I was about to spend the rest of the evening with. Back then, they all had skinheads; today, they have evolved and have unkempt long hair bobs and look like dinner ladies. Back then, I looked like a dinner lady. Now I have a skinhead and look like a 90s scall. Is there something in that? Who knows? Back to this night; my unacquainted surroundings had started to make me nervous, as this did not play to the narrative these new friends had been waxing lyrical about. Was this really going to be the night that would change my life forever, in a good way? Down the line, I could see it would in a bad way, most definitely!

By the time I arrived, the event had started. There was that thumping sound I experienced when queuing up at the Academy. It sounded tribal, but it was coming out of this building called Fallows, which had no windows, and the music was louder than I have ever heard. Surrounded by these ninjas, the natives kept calling each other "Lad" or "Kidda" from out of the hoods of their Berghaus coats. Did they REALLY not know each other's first names, I thought? How could you differentiate when one called out "Lad" to another? Will they all turn around? And why did they spit after every sentence? It wasn't normal gollying, it was little hisses of phlegm. If you closed your eyes momentarily, you could have been in a tropical jungle surrounded by nocturnal insects. All you could hear was "psst" and "hsst" as they sprinkled each other with phlegm. It was odd; it was like wild moggies marking their territory: each other. A rabbit in the headlights, I was now rubbing shoulders with these scalls. I have never been so close to so many; I was not ready to fight; I was ready to take flight.

Chapter 22

Billy Whizz - Amphetamine

I couldn't take flight as I had nowhere to go, at least without parting this sea of Berghaus ninjas. I didn't know whether they were going to rob me or open me up. How on earth was this going to be a night of pure joy, exhilaration, and euphoria? I was petrified and was going nowhere, other than through the entrance of the club, which I was now closer to and at the point of no return. The only comfort I had; the people I had arrived with were as calm as Hindu cows; their countenance had not changed once; this was normal to them. I just looked at my feet and allowed my perm to fall over my face in case what I was feeling on the inside was manifesting itself on the outside. I hadn't arrived yet, but I couldn't wait to leave. I assumed the only reason these scalls had been so mild-tempered so far was because of the beast on the door. In fact, there were several, all dressed in black with bomber Jackets and black leather gloves, patrolling the oncoming herd of ninjas. The doors these days were run by the fathers and uncles and big brothers of these ninjas, the underworld, Liverpool's gangsters, and their families. If one of them thought you looked too shady, you would be dragged out of the queue and sent on your way.

Once inside, the night was well and truly underway, but it was still early, and the street ninjas had taken up their parochial positions in their respective corners of the club, depending on what area of Liverpool they were from, East, South or North. They would congregate with their Berghaus coats on. This wasn't a coat; it was a uniform. Let's be clear here; this was a sweaty rave. It was dripping off the ceiling. When the lights dropped, a dandruff-exposing fluorescent strip light would reveal the whites of their eyes from the shadow of their hoods. It looked like a wolf pack patrolling their next live meal, ME! Staying close to my new friends was the only comfort I had in this loud unfamiliar edge of a very uncomfortable, uncharted part of the world. I say edge; it felt like I was about to step off into the abyss. I was in the middle of an industrial estate in the back end of beyond, in a place that felt like no other, miles away from home, to which no bus or train came near. I now didn't have enough money to run and jump a taxi as I had just given most of my cash to Ged, one of my Hindu cow-like friends, who had now disappeared into the midst of one of these tribal Berghaus corners. He was away to do some business with one of these street urchins. Tonight, I was on a strict diet of champagne. This was not any normal champagne, this was pink champagne, and it was not fluidified; it came as a powder.

Living on the edge of my nerves, I saw the little parcel of narcotics was on its way over to me, a drug I had never taken before. What on earth was I thinking? My heart was racing, and my hands had become clammy. I could not calm myself. I don't know if it was the environment that I was now in or the fact I was about to consume this evil demonic drug cut with rat poison and embalming fluid that could give me a heart attack or brain damage. This new acquaintance from college was now unceremoniously shaking my hand as if he was a brother from another mother I had not seen for years. It was strange. It wasn't a normal handshake. He grabbed my hand diagonally, then gripped the inside of my fingers as if he was using my hand to open an invisible door. Despite a few repositions, it seemed never-ending. When was he going to let go and give me back my hand? It was now dancing to the tune of his, almost to the beat of the deafening music? He kept winking at me, which seemed equally odd; was it a twitch? It was incessant, and he was using the whole side of his face to exaggerate this wink, still doing somersaults with my fingers. I just winked back.

Then he let go of my hand. I then realised why he was winking so hard: he had impregnated the palm of my hand with a little wrap of paper, which was an inch long and a centimetre wide. It felt like a piece of Wrigley's spearmint chewing gum, but it wasn't. It was narcotics. I quickly pocketed the wrap of amphetamine, better known as Speed, known locally as Billy. I had to decide if I was about to become part of this chemical generation. I was certainly closer than I had ever been.

(Amphetamine is a psychostimulant drug that is known to produce increased wakefulness and focus. Some people crush it up and snort it or dab it onto their gums. Some people roll it up in cigarette paper and swallow it like a capsule: this is called 'bombing'. It can be mixed into drinks. If only I had known this back then.)

I had finally plucked up the courage to navigate my way to the toilets with this parcel of pink powder. It had been sitting in my pocket for close to an hour as the debate raged in my head, should I, shouldn't I. When I wasn't telling myself this could be rat poison, I was wondering, what if I had a heart attack? The first time I took drugs, I threw a whitey and spewed everywhere; what was going to happen to me this time? I was not going to touch this stuff until I knew the others had come up on theirs, and I was sure they still had a pulse and weren't rolling around on the floor convulsing, trying not to swallow their tongues. I couldn't hide the fact that I hadn't taken mine. In part, they understood; they knew it was my first time. I was way out of my comfort zone, observing these new friends now bouncing around me like Duracell bunnies. I could not escape the stark reality; I was in the lion's den, carrying illegal drugs in my pocket, Class B. I checked before arrival, knowing a bit of 'Billy' would be on the menu, and it carried a 5-year prison sentence for possession. In my naivety, this was what I was getting if I was caught with this wrap. I had two options, throw it on the floor or neck it. After being assured I wasn't going to die by my new friends, "It's not going to kill you" did not ease the anxiety. Until that point, I didn't know death was an option. You can reconcile comfort; for example, you will not be sick, or you won't faint. To say I will not die, in my mind, meant such an extreme was now a distinct possibility. Regardless, I had to make up my mind. At least, I was now heading to the toilet to consider the matter further, which meant when I arrived, I would be closer to consuming these narcotics, at least compared to when I was standing scared stiff in the club, having a mental arm-wrestle with my yin and yang.

Now sat in a cubicle, I had one hand holding the door where the lock once was, and the other this wrap. I sat there for what felt like an eternity. I was getting pins and needles in my feet. Suddenly, I heard several thuds on the door. Who was it, a doorman? The police? This extra edge did help me focus. It's now or never. There goes that thud again 'bang bang'. Now I couldn't unload that powder into my mouth fast enough. Pouring it into my mouth was like swallowing a tablespoon of self-raising flour. The only thing now self-raising was how anxious and scared I had become. The only way I could get this Class B drug into my oesophagus was by summoning up as much saliva and mucus as possible so that I then could re-swallow, dragging the amphetamine kicking and screaming away from my mouth and into my gut. I had given up trying to generate saliva, and this stuff tasted like battery acid. I felt like I was choking, and this guy (a Berghaus ninja it turned out) on the other side of the door would not shut up. I had to leave, head bowed, my perm hanging over my face. Like a dog with rabies, I was frothing at the mouth. No sooner had I left the drug throne behind than I was necking the tap faucet. Ouch, it was the hot water tap, but I didn't care. The deadly deed was finally done.

What I experienced, was the gateway to every other narcotic experience thereafter, or rather a promotion to Class A drugs. It is safe to say that when I arrived back at the edge of the dance floor, my crew couldn't be more pleased; I had finally dropped. I needed a drink: "I'm away to get an orange!" "Noooooo, vitamin C kills the buzz." "What buzz?" I thought. I still had a backup plan if things started to go awry; copious amounts of pure orange would be necked to bring me down if I ever got up. Ten minutes passed, I felt nothing, 20 minutes passed, no change. Did I lose most of it when I was panic-swallowing? I was convinced I had been sold baking soda. Thirty minutes passed, but still, nothing. One part of me was in denial, and the other doing its best to convince me there's a tingle rising up from my little toe. Then, all of a sudden, I'm bobbing like an empty dinghy in a storm. I can't keep my hands still. Did I just cock my hand like a gun and pretend to shoot the ceiling? My body was now fizzing. I knew something had changed because I couldn't feel the back of my neck anymore no matter how hard I rubbed it, and Uncle Remus had shrank to three times his normal size. Goosebumps everywhere: they call it 'rushing.' I knew I was in full throttle because I was now on a podium doing big fish, little fish, trying to bite my ear in between intermittent fist bumps with every Berghaus ninja within reach. "Wait until I tell Dave and The Bumper!" I thought, "they must have a bit of this!"

I had gone from extreme fear, pining for Mr Bear, hot milk, and Farley's rusk in the safety of my scratcher, to dancing on a stage swapping sweat with my new Berghaus brothers, wishing it would never end. My body electrified from head to toe as this exhilarating drug poured into every fibre of my existence. I knew right there and then what we realised in the Academy in that chill-out room; it was all about the buzz of the drugs. I wanted more. I was going to have more; what next?

Chapter 23

Who is Gary & Charlie? Where is Billy?

Returning home, reeling from my latest hedonistic adventure, it was now in the early hours of Tuesday morning. The effects of the amphetamine had swallowed five hours of my life, and it hadn't let up yet, although I was on a come-down. I was wide awake with my eyes wide shut. My senses fell into overdrive. Thoughts about nothing would race through my mind. I didn't want to alert my parents that I was high on drugs. Would I wake up in time to go to college the next day? To not go would increase my parents' suspicion. I already had the Spanish inquisition, "Why are you going out on a Monday night? Who are these new friends?" Sleeping felt like an impossibility. I was wired, and my body was buzzing like tinnitus through a megaphone. In the dark quiet of my room, my thoughts were inwardly deafening, keeping me wide awake. Closing my eyes heightened the white noise I was hearing, like the amplified hum of an exposed power cable. On the surface of my eyeball, I could feel my blood coursing through the veins of my eyelids, and my heart felt like it was bouncing on the top of my chest. I could feel my pulse without pressing a vein, throbbing in my brain and when I wasn't sucking on my teeth, I couldn't stop chewing my tongue, which was now sticking to the top of my mouth like velcro. In ever-increasing pulses, a surge would rush through me, inadvertently compelling my body to quiver. I had to stretch out my fingers and hands to release hypertension. I glanced at my face in the mirror on my bedside table, lit up only by the streetlights invading the dark of my room. I looked like a startled cotton-mouthed owl, an image all the stranger due to my jazz hands turrets. I involuntarily kept twitching. The only saving grace was that no one could see me.

I couldn't bear my crawling skin. It was clammy and felt sticky. The static between my bedsheets and flesh was agitating. In the end, I gave up trying to sleep, got back in the saddle and let it ride. Quite clearly, I was still enduring the effects. Whilst the drugs no longer compelled me to action physically, my mind was quite literally bouncing off the walls of my skull. Ordinarily, when I was kept awake, my thoughts were consumed with dread and fear. Other than the quieting fear of Mum waking up and walking in, I didn't worry about the world; it was almost enjoyable. I was comfortably high, albeit in an unusual temporal position of positivity borne out of a sense of misplaced achievement. In my mind, I had just done serious drugs, had the night of my life, did not die, and wasn't sick. I had taken what seemed like the biggest risk of my life so far, and it paid off. I soon settled with the realisation that I no longer wanted to sleep. In fact, I could not wait for morning and college to meet up with my nomadic friends and revisit last night. I managed to get two hours of sleep and drag myself to college. By the day's end, I was that spent I would have struggled to drag a sleeping cat off a greasy glass coffee table. Safe to say, no sooner had my head hit the pillow that night than pixies were dancing around it.

I waxed lyrical to Dave about my Monday night experience but soon realised there is a world of difference threatening to take drugs compared to partaking. It came as no surprise when it was Dave's turn. He was having second thoughts. "Dave, would I give you anything that would kill you?" Mentioning death and drugs in the same sentence, or the devilment of my promise not to kill him was enough; did he trust me that much? In any event, we were back on track heading to the bus that would transport Dave closer to becoming part of this chemical generation I had so unceremoniously joined seven days before. I thought convincing Dave was the hard part; then I realised I now needed to buy the same drugs I had coerced Dave to take.

I entered the nearest darkened corner of the club, shoulder-deep in ninjas. "You after Gary?" Was he speaking to me? He was looking at me. Whilst I breathed a momentary sigh of relief, I did wonder if it was mistaken identity, as I didn't know anybody called Gary. Politely I said "no" and moved on. "Gary's in the house." There it is again, who the @@@@! is Gary? This wasn't the same ninja I spoke to seconds ago. Was he Mr Big? I had two options: backpack it out of this jungle, or find out who Gary is and did he have any Billy? The next time I was offered the chance to meet Gary, I would let his minion know I'm here to do business. No sooner had I made this inward decree, almost on cue, "Ya after Gary, lad?" "Yes, but for Billy!" The ninja paused momentarily, unsure if I was trying to make a fool of him. Trust me; I wasn't! Unwrinkling his confused face, he then replied, "Got no Billy, lad, but what about Charlie?" What happened to Gary and who is Charlie? Another dealer, Gary's business partner? Fearing I couldn't make any more of a fool of myself, I passed on meeting Charlie, politely made my excuses, and moved on. Now I was the one confused; should I be dealing with Gary or Charlie? I wanted Billy! I couldn't go back to Dave empty-handed, as I had him by a thread on a tenterhook. Any hiccup may change his persuaded position. There it was again: "You after Gary?" I had to have one more shot, so I declared in no uncertain terms, "I'm after Billy!" This time, I uttered it out of the side of my mouth, exaggerating my accent to sound like I was a hardened individual that wasn't about to accept £20 worth of baking soda. "How many?" said the ninja. Result! This must be Gary! Finally, we meet. "Two wraps," I declared. I handed over Dave's and my tenners, and the deal was done. I never got to meet Charlie, but I had just completed my first drug deal, and Dave was going to have some. It was later that I learned "Gary" was slang for a former football player, whose surname was Ablet. Ablet sounded like a tablet. When I was asked if I am after "Gary," they were referring to Ecstasy tablets. I also learnt that Charlie was the first name of a character whose second name was White, referring to the colour of cocaine and was code for the same. It's a good job LSD was not on offer, as that was referred to as Larry, and MDMA, the purer form of the same found in Ecstasy, was known as Mandy. Gary, Charlie, Larry, Mandy, and Billy! I couldn't wait to leave this land of name confusion. All I wanted to do at the time, was get high.

Let me introduce you to another one of my partners in crime, Hiawatha. Most evenings in my bedroom, under the foil of the scent of what my parents thought were joss sticks, we would smoke cannabis. Sometimes it was skunk or cabbage, which was chemically illuminated weed, which kicked out a horrendous thick compost smell. I can imagine when that thick weed smell hit my Mums nostrils, turning to Dad and saying, "he's got those blooming joss sticks on again." On these nights, we would be 'stoned immaculate,' a phrase made famous by the Lizard King himself, Jim Morrison. However, we would usually end up under the spell of famine-like starvation, our stomachs touching our backs, even though a few hours earlier we had eaten a full evening meal. This was the hunger-induced state brought on by cannabis, known as the 'Munchies.' Our Bob Geldof was Pizza Reaction, a takeaway who would come to our starvation salvation. This very special food parcel would comprise a folded large garlic bread with cheese, thick mozzarella, which was textured like Hubba Bubba, quite simply a party in your mouth, with an en-tray of chilli and garlic ribs.

One-night The Bumper couldn't partake, he sacked the lads for a girl, which always had repercussions, if one of us was not there. So, it was open season on the absentee, the opportunity to extract the wet stuff at the others expense. On this occasion we got the Yellow Pages, (a directory of all Liverpool business telephone numbers) and phoned many professional businesses, such as Accountants and Solicitors, knowing they were closed, and we would get their answering machines. We left the following message, "This is Charlie White, I am looking for some advice, please call me back at your earliest convenience," followed by The Bumpers telephone number. Knowing these messages would be picked up early in the morning when The Bumper would still be in his scratcher giving it zzzzzd's. The thought of The Bumpers mum fielding calls all morning asking if Charlie White was available had us in stitches, and then the same when we learnt that he got the third degree dragged up out of his lie-in with his bed still on his back, "Lee whose this Charlie White, all I've done all morning is take calls asking for Charlie." It would have been a picture watching Lee rub the sleep out of his eyes wondering if he was still asleep dreaming and why was his mum banging on about Charlie, also trying to conceal his inadvertent guilt as he knew, what his mum didn't, it meant cocaine.

Safe to say if you were absent from a sesh, you were getting it. On one occasion when the weed ran out, we decided to collect the Pizza's as opposed to delivery. The Bumper and I offered to pick the food up. Upon returning out of nowhere a fully made spliff appeared. It was claimed some left over weed had been unearthed. As we had offered to pick up the Pizzas, The Bumper and I were given the first drags on this suspicious spliff. Little did we know the colourless plant that had shrivelled up dead in its pot on the windowsill had been separated from its dry crispy leaves, which were now sprinkled into this spliff The Bumper and I were chonging. Dead funny we thought. The main culprit got his comeuppance, as the next time he was in our company and we were having a sesh he was getting it.

Embarrassingly, on this very special night of revenge The Bumper and I stood on our tip toes trimming our love bushes, cutting off a spliff's worth. Quite a dangerous manoeuvre, as we were sniggering trying not to laugh out loud and alert Hiawatha next door who was waiting for this very special Indian peace pipe to arrive (this is how he got his name). We were literally shaking with laughter as Uncle Remus was getting a short back and sides, one wrong move could have ended up with one of us being inadvertently circumcised. We wrapped this hairy tinder up and no sooner did it look like a spliff we passed it to the unbeknown but deserving recipient. We then sat back and watched Hiawatha suck the colour out of his face relighting it for the fourth time and sucking this phat blunt dry, smoking at least a third of this hairy cigar, the cigarette paper had turned brown because Hiawatha had burnt it that much trying to re-light it.

Chapter 24

LSD – Lysergic Acid Diethylamide

It was now summertime and college was coming to an end for the third year. I still had GCSEs on my mind, and whilst the pressure to succeed and meet my parents' minimum expectations had become less important, at least to me, it was my fourth attempt if you included the failed attempt at school. But I had yet another plan. My hair was now very long and past my shoulders, and I had gotten an Aiwa Walkman that Christmas. This was "state of the art." The headphones had a remote control from which I could inconspicuously play, pause and fast forward or rewind the tape in my pocket. Before you sit exams, you are given past exam papers to practise and ordinarily, the teachers would often drop hints on what to revise and what might feature in that year's exams. I had come up with a plan to dictate answers to likely questions and record them onto a tape, which I would control from my pocket during the exam listening through one earbud, hidden by my long hair. To my utter amazement, it worked a treat; I got four Cs and one B. Five GCSEs! Can you believe it? Whilst I could not be educated or understand most of the subject matter, I had enough ingenuity to cheat, and do it well, which was a damn sight better than a fake certificate. To the college, this new certificate was real and meant I could legitimately now stay on to finalise my A levels.

The time for Larks in The Parks had arrived, a free event held yearly in Sefton Park, a music festival in Liverpool featuring local bands and DJs. I had convinced Dave and The Bumper that we should attend and take a trip, another new experience, but this time we would increase the risk. It would be a Class A drug. The trip we were about to take was a Rainbow, as it had the image of one on its surface. Interestingly, these were only £3 per trip. What we were effectively buying was a small paper tab that had been soaked in LSD, often referred to as acid. As a class A drug, it's illegal to have for yourself, give away or sell. Possession can get you up to 7 years in prison, an unlimited fine, or both. Supplying someone else, even your friends, can get you life in prison. Unlike the momentary dread I felt before taking Speed and being caught and then imprisoned, I had experienced multiple nights on Speed or smoking weed, breaking the law, and not getting caught. Even though I was about to advance to a class A drug, I had no problem throwing caution to the wind. I was becoming indifferent, despite the overstated threats of prison. A life sentence? Really? I thought it would never happen to me. I knew that going to jail for taking these drugs was unlikely, even though I was effectively now supplying and selling them to my friends. I was ready to step up my pursuit.

We headed out together, excited for a new adventure, ready for a new Class A experience. When we arrived, the crowd had begun to gather, so we set off nearby, but not too visible that we could not conspire on how and when to take these trips. We had decided before we left that we would take half, and intricately cut these squared tabs diagonally and put them back into the sealed plastic pocket we stored them in. There was certainly a degree of anxiety and uncertainty because we knew this was Class A. (Those who say weed is not a gateway drug, do not know what they are talking about... Trust me.)

We each placed a paper half-tab onto our tongues. We did not swallow, as we were led to believe the acid gets into your system quicker by being dissolved on your tongue. So, we agitated this little paper tab around our mouths until it was no more and then waited in nervous anticipation. In equal measure, we were excited. We were told that after 20 minutes, the trip would begin. We decided to take a look around some of the stalls whilst we remained in control of our faculties. We soon realised half an hour had passed, and we felt absolutely nothing. Consequently, we agreed to take the other half. In for a penny, in for a pound. Lee had bumped into some old school friends; Dave and I saw this as an opportunity to go to nearby Lark Lane and get some refreshments.

No sooner had we left the grassed area of the park than the acid kicked in. We stepped over a speed hump with yellow markings, which seemed to grow as we hovered above it, and the yellow lines started to come alive. I looked at Dave and said, "Did you see that?" Dave concurred. However, I just shook my head as if to clear it, like you always do when you take drugs. Inwardly, when you're not convinced something is happening, you think you've been sold a dud. Then you are wondering if the slightest nuance or unacquainted experience was the start of the buzz. We carried on to Lark Lane and entered the newsagents. No sooner had I stepped from outside to inside than something shifted in my reality. It felt like the walls were closing in on me. I was now fighting an inward battle to act normal and resist, if possible, the obvious shift in my consciousness. The same was happening to Dave as I watched him trying to also act normal and, in doing so, outwardly acting anything but. Whilst I continued to convince myself my mind was simply playing tricks, I was now conscious of the fact I was being watched. I proceeded to do the most normal thing I could and buy a drink. No sooner had I carried this bottle of juice to the counter than for absolutely no reason, I started to laugh out loud, uncontrollably. This was not a giggle; it was hysterics, fighting for breath, almost swallowing my tongue and side-splitting, bent over holding my knees with snot coming out of each nostril and tears streaming down my cheeks. I was a mess, and couldn't even speak to buy the drink. I had to leave. It was official; we were 'tripping'. We now felt an overwhelming sense of brotherhood and quite clearly a man down, who we had to get back to and save. We were incomplete without The Bumper, and we could not settle until we were together again. We found Lee on his back, pointing at the sky. Together we now felt safe, completed by our reunion and unity. It was us versus the world. We would not step out of this hallucinogenic circle of trust and acid brotherhood; this threesome had now become one, but in the visceral sense only.

It is impossible to fully relay this experience of being completely out of your mind, but I share my experiences, including the description that follows, not for glorification's sake, rather so you may understand the affects drugs have. I share, to explain why - despite the ugly sensations experienced when the user initially enters through the counterfeit 'spiritual gateway' - so many, young people in particular, are drawn to taking them. Here goes...

The colours seemed many times brighter, and the sounds many times sharper. Everything that moved now had a sound; you could hear a leaf fall or fly by, and a spider spit out its web or an insect crawl across a stone. The music from the DJ tent was unlike any sound I have ever heard before. It was like hearing the same music for the very first time, as if before I had been partially deaf. I could wave my hand across my face, and I would get trail backs where I could see multiple hands, one chasing the other. As the vision of the first hand faded, the next one came to life. I could hear the wind blowing through the trees. One of us would declare a revelation like, "I can hear the grass grow," the others would unanimously agree. It was as if by saying it, it happened. Our words would activate the weird, wonderful, and the strange, making the unbelievable believable. It was sensory overload. We had several hours ahead whereby we would go deeper, which was thought-provoking until we couldn't remember what we were about to say, or if we were speaking out loud, in our heads, or at all, and if another was trying to speak or be spoken to. It was as if the world disappeared, and it was just us three in this parallel universe, the one that made the mundane world we had left behind. The overwhelming sense of being in the middle of this trip almost began to thicken like a fog around us, but without losing clarity of what our eyes could see or ears could hear. My body began to feel numb, yet I could still feel every hair on my arm, move in the breeze. We bumped into Shakehands. He knew straight away we were off our heads. This was the wrong time to try and hold a normal conversation with another who was quite obviously not on the same wavelength. The downside of this drug was that it often led to paranoia. In a moment, visually, I came out of my body, yet my feet had not left the ground. It was an experience I can only describe as floating tunnel vision. I was up above, and Shakehands was on the ground. It felt like I was 40 feet in the air. I was in the thick of this trip and was seeing things that were not there, or at the very least, were very exaggerated; but it was still coming in waves to the point I started to feel like I was no longer in control. We were absolutely wired but having the time of our lives. I knew I had lost control, so why fight it? I had this overwhelming sense of release to simply buzz, be free and do what I want. I believed in this alternative technicolour state of mind and universe with my three best mates, Lee, Dave, and Gareth, who had died when I was six, but was now alive again as a result of this trip. These were the sort of things that could be brought to life in your mind.

We began tripping regularly, and I have numerous tales to tell, but the next two are the most extreme. We had arranged another night in. This time, we were taking Greenshields. Once we had dropped these trips, we headed off to the nearest graveyard for extra effect. In the darkness on this cold and windy night, I lost the lads, as Shotgun and Harvey - another passing ship in the night - had joined us. I could not find them. I am short-sighted but wouldn't wear glasses, so I could not see them in the distance. It was too windy, so I could not hear them. This trip was in full flow, and I had given up my pursuit of the gang on my way out of the graveyard by myself in the dark. Now however, I was seeing corpses coming up out of their graves! Convinced I was being chased by dead bodies, absolutely petrified, I ran like a 100m sprinter. When Scooby-Doo enters into a chase, he momentarily goes nowhere as his legs spin in circles, then flies off the screen like a missile. But it felt like a lifetime, waiting for the ejection point from this on-the-spot sprint I had entered into. I was really scared. The best way to describe what I felt, took me back to when I was a kid. If I woke up in the middle of the night and went downstairs to get a drink, I would run back to bed as fast as possible as if being chased by rats. Unless I was in my bed, feet off the ground, I was not safe. Only once under the covers would the chasing red-eye rats disappear. This was what it was like as an adult on this trip. Although in your mind you could see rats, they were not really there. And although I could see these corpses, they were a figment of my imagination.

By the time I had returned home, it was sometime after the gang turned up they found comfort rubbing my arm, rocking back and forth. However, no sooner had we regrouped than I was fine, so we headed back into the night, this time to the nearest park, where we spent the rest of the night convinced a 50-foot tree was Big Bird of Sesame Street.

We had many other amazingly weird experiences and took many more trips on the variety of different drugs available. The most outrageous thing we did on one of these expeditions into our minds was climbing up a derelict high-rise residential building. If that wasn't bad enough, we proceeded to carelessly traverse the edge of the flat, open-roof on a significantly windy night, without a thought of the imminent death-fall below if we lost balance. Whilst the thought never crossed my mind, we did hear stories of individuals jumping off roofs on LSD thinking they could fly. We were surely dicing with death. In terms of outwardly taking an unprecedented risk, this couldn't be any closer. As I write this, I am absolutely convinced the odds were stacked against us living beyond that night, particularly at the moment we thought it was acceptable to jump across an open lift-shaft in the dark, with a 200-foot drop. Absolutely crazy! If there was a God, He was surely protecting me - us - that night. Back then, I didn't give this a moments thought. I was now ready for the pinnacle.

Chapter 25

Ecstasy

Methylenedioxymethamphetamine

(MDMA)

We knew that ecstasy 'E' was the one and only synergistic partner of rave, without taking it. We had been high and in love with the scene, but we had never been high and 'Loved Up'. Apparently, during the 90s, at its peak, on average 500,000 tablets were consumed weekly in the UK. What made this drug special, so popular, and why was it unlike any other? What was the attraction? The Oxford dictionary defines ecstasy as an overwhelming feeling of joy or rapture, an emotional or religious frenzy. There's that close association with the church again; Ekstasis, the Greek and the etymological root of the word ecstasy defines it as standing outside of oneself. Again, on the theme alluding to a spiritual experience, how else could standing outside oneself be described, or did this have a more sinister meaning?

Had we forgotten what it was like to be free? Were we were ever free at all? The religious church says we were all born sick. Is this a social disease or biblical disposition to be born into sin? The church believed it is only sin that separates us from experiencing the ecstasy of heaven above and on earth. Was E a counterfeit back-door experience to this heavenly realm, a supernatural experience of Love, now paid upfront, without sacrifice, and without giving up sin? What does it mean to be 'Loved Up'? Was it simply a happy pill, able to release me into a synthetic feeling of love, or was it the removal of the stain of life to expose true love for yourself and mankind? Is this the love we once had, but we allowed life and the things done to us to cover it up and hide it away? Was it, in fact, love at all? What is real love? Here's one version: *'Love is patient, love is kind. It does not envy, it does not boast, it is not proud. It does not dishonour others, it is not self-seeking, it is not easily angered, it keeps no record of wrongs. Love does not delight in evil but rejoices with the truth. It always protects, always trusts, always hopes, always perseveres. Love never fails. (1 Corinthians 13:4-8).* Can one little tablet really do all this?

Where did it come from, and how did E get into my hands? E's journey of discovery began well before it arrived on the rave scene and lit up a generation. It was first synthesised and used in the First World War as an appetite suppressant to control hunger during battle and energise the troops. It was also used in therapy sessions for traumatised soldiers. Interestingly, 75% of the subjects expressed a desire for peace and an end to war, with several talking of loving everyone, including the enemy. In the 1950s, military researchers experimented with it as a disorientation drug, taking the fight out of the soldier, replacing it with peace and love, effectively making the enemy vulnerable and easier to defeat by emotionally and physiologically disarming the opposition. It's the modern story of the use of MDMA that brought it to the dance floor. It was rediscovered in the 1960s by a biochemist pursuing an interest in psychedelia, as a study, with the biochemist as the lab rat. In the late 70s and early 80s, it gained the nickname Adam. There it is again, another biblical association. It was called Adam because of its hedonistic rebirth-like qualities. Interestingly, it was also being used in marriage therapy and psychoanalysis. Apparently, a 5-hour MDMA trip could help the patient work through emotional blockages that would have otherwise taken five months of weekly sessions. By the early 80s, a fully-fledged Ecstasy scene existed in the US, but they called it 'X', and it became very popular as a legal high. In 1985, it was banned. In the

UK, it was already a class A illegal drug, alongside heroin and cocaine. But of course, E ultimately proved to have one other infinitely more alluring application. When clubbers fell under its spell listening to rave music in the nightclub, it turned fighters into lovers, strangers into best friends, and created a total atmosphere of intimacy. More poignantly put, a blissful merger with something larger than the paltry isolate of me, myself, and I. For a season, MDMA was a miracle cure for the English disease of emotional constipation, reserve, and inhibition. E quite literally wiped out football hooliganism overnight. They would hug each other rather than fight.

It seemed to make total sense that our next narcotic night of naughtiness would be through E. MDMA clearly had an identity of its own, a remarkable chemical combining the sensory intensification and auditory enhancement of weed and low-dose LSD, the sleep-defying energy-boosting effects of Speed, and the uninhibited conviviality of alcohol. Dave, The Bumper, The Shotgun and I had done all the above, so it seemed a natural transition to do it again, but in one pill, particularly if the combined result produced the outpouring of empathy and love never felt or experienced before, otherwise known as being 'Loved Up.' I expected it to be at the very least artificial sanity that temporarily quietened my neurotic self; but would it free me from anxiety and fear, and light up my senses? My 20th birthday couldn't have been a more fitting night to take this Ecstasy leap of faith. I say, 'leap of faith,' because there was still a lot of mystique around this one, and of course, the press had gone to town, describing it as anything but a love-filled experience. They associated it more closely with the demonic. It was also relatively new, unlike weed and LSD, which had been around since the 60s, and Speed since the 70s; at least for general consumption in the way E had become in the early 90s. Also, you didn't know what you were going to get. You were either going to have the best night of your life; or the worst. The latter is less frequent and known as sledging. This did play heavily on my mind, because I had seen people when they sledged, and it was not a pretty sight. It was probably this that gave birth to the media demon-fuelled narrative because it was as if the person had quite literally been possessed. Interestingly, some say mind-altering drugs give access to the spiritual realm, but not the edifying one referred to in the Bible. In fact, the sufferer would experience the polar opposite. Love would be replaced by self and anger, excitement by fear, calmness by anxiety, attentiveness and liveliness by a complete physical breakdown as panic set in, and fear of dying; usually requiring ambulance attendance. I recall seeing to two girls were literally climbing the walls; they looked like they had been possessed. They were well-presented and eye candy, but now they looked totally different: insane, their faces contorted, on their knees feeling the walls on the drugs I sold to them..

I had started getting more into the techno side of rave music, as opposed to just House. It was basically more electronic, faster beats, and less singing. As it was my birthday, I got to choose the venue. We went to The Hard Dock, which was effectively a former tobacco warehouse in the middle of nowhere, converted into a techno nightclub. This was as close as I got to an illegal rave. It was just a warehouse with a smoke machine, some lights, and a strobe. It was all about the music and the drugs. This place solely relied on the Ecstasy buzz; otherwise, it would have been scary, certainly very aggressive, with plenty of gratuitous violence. It gave the place an extra edge. It felt like stepping into satan's den, the lion's den whilst it was awake but spiked with this love drug. You didn't want to be around after twilight, or more particularly when the drugs had worn off, and the natives had returned to their original state. This added to the thrill and the risk, and therefore, the reward. It's a little bit like parachute jumpers. They know it's dangerous, but do it anyway for the buzz.

Thankfully, Shakehands was with us. He knew who sold the best Gary's. This time, I was going to follow and watch where he went and who he spoke to. He made his way through the several waves of ninjas. He stopped in front of his destination, who was a unit: he had a chin like

Desperate Dan, and despite wearing a string vest which looked like it had been purchased from Mothercare, he was clearly not someone to be messed with. We called him Jaws. I now knew who to go to next time. I assumed he would be there; he was. I remember later dealing, getting fake £20 notes. In the dark of the nightclub, it was difficult to check for authenticity. When I went to The Hard Dock, I would palm the fake notes off on Jaws, dangerously bold, in fact ludicrously stupid. I suspect he didn't expect to be ripped off by little old me, which was exactly what I did. The tablets he was selling on my birthday were called Double Deckers. The name was derived from the fact that this was a thick tablet, like two small tablets together. Shakehands, in typical fashion, handed it over with one of his handshakes. In no time at all, it was in my gullet, being chased by something wet and fizzy. I was all in and about to be taken out of control. All I could do was hold on.

Chapter 26

MC Cosmic

MC stands for Master of Ceremonies. At a rave, he is better known as a lyrical gangster who chants rap over the DJ's mix, like an orchestra's conductor. But this MC performed to the drugs coursing through the ravers' veins, raising the highs, anointing the airwaves, telling us the rush was coming in and up, and when to put your hands in the air. He, the rave evangelist, directs his congregation. His primary responsibilities were to unify the dancers, set the tempo, and shape the sound mixed by the DJ, all done through the sound of his voice. The MC at this place was called Cosmic. I wondered whether his immediate presence had intentionally cornered me. Was he the reason I started to feel so uneasy? As he walked up to me, I could tell he was agitated. He looked like he had a fire in his eyes and his dreads swung through the air with every bounce and step he made in my direction. They looked like Medusa's children: had his snakeheads turned me to stone? I was like a statue and couldn't move; was I under his spell? He brushed past me. I then realised he had his sights set on the arcade machine behind me. I was in his way; regardless, he still looked me up and down, in and out, with his reptilian eyes. Could he hear my every thought? Was he really there? Of course, he was; he had just put his 50p into the arcade machine. He started playing. Why so aggressively? Stuck to the spot, I didn't want to move yet at the same time, I didn't want to be near this predator.

It was all part of the ecstasy ride. The beginning was over. Like being on the big dipper, I was now at the highest point, about to be launched into the centre of this journey from a not-so-great height. I didn't feel great. The anticipation started to swell up within me, as did the surge and effects of the chemicals now taking hold and kicking like a mule. I felt nauseous, lethargic, fearful, and an unpleasant heaviness seemed to be darkening my soul. An uncomfortable presence surrounded me. Was it demonic? "Is this really an MC, or is it satan himself?" I thought. Coming up on what I had just dropped, I was not yet deep enough. I couldn't question if this was for real or just a figment of my imagination. But I was struggling to separate fact from fiction, reality from fantasy and in my case, safety from this impending nightmare. I was in a fight I could not win. It felt like a battle I was losing. Why was he smashing the buttons of the arcade machine so hard, each time harder than before, and growling at the screen? It was unnecessary but captivating. So, I watched him act out the moves physically that he was playing electronically, restrained only by the need to keep his hands connected to the joypad. I've never seen a body jerk and convulse so much without moving its arms. I wanted to remove my gaze from him, but I was transfixed. Sure, he wanted me to see him. I felt like he was giving me no choice. Did he need me to see what he was about to do and make me an accessory to the fact? Then time stopped, slow motion kicked in, MC Cosmic pulled back his elbow like he was lining up an arrow in a bow, and with a clenched fist, he released his knuckle-pointed weapon into the centre of the arcade screen, obliterating it. He pulled his fist out of this machine, now with bloody splinters of glass embedded in his knuckles. Like a disco ball, it glistened as it reflected the backdrop of the dance floor light show. Then his eyes returned to mine. His piercing gaze led me to believe we were in it together, co-conspirators, and if I uttered a word of what he had just done, he was coming for me. He spun 180 degrees, his dreads flared up for extra effect like a frilled-necked lizard, and he returned to where he once came. Having gone, he was still in my mind. Were we connected telepathically, demonically? Thoughts were now exaggerating the brain-freeze in my head. The fear I could not control was eating me up.

I had entered into a drug-induced alternative state of consciousness, one that was not playing to the love-bug narrative. Did I just meet satan, and was I now possessed? I wasn't sure. My body had begun to reject the poison I had swallowed 30 minutes earlier. My hands had become sweaty, my skin clammy, my heart felt like it kept stopping. Was I flatlining? I didn't want to be here anymore! Was I sledging? My mind was now full of visions of contorted people. Dread was stealing my every thought, taking my mind captive. The darkness of the club had become oppressive and unsettling, conjuring up flashbacks of that time in the graveyard. Similarly, Dave, The Bumper and The Shotgun were nowhere to be seen. Like a snail recoils into its shell under threat, I had regressed into a dark corner of this club for safety, with only a brick wall corner to my back, so I knew no one was behind me. I kept looking, just in case. I stole a moment to get my head together, but I felt like it was about to roll off my shoulders. I was lost to my friends, which could happen in a club this big and dark. The trauma from the graveyard was repeating itself right there in that nightclub. This time there was nothing friend or foe could do to stop me from falling, plummeting further into the dark abyss, now way too deep, so the only way I hoped was up. I had an overwhelming need to leave and escape. I was being drawn to the light. If I could just get to the chillout room at the other end of the club! It seemed to be groaning on my behalf, beckoning me into its shelter. I was certain the light was the cure to the oppressive dark state that had now overcome and consumed me. I needed to leave where I was and get to the chillout room ASAP. Every step I took felt like I sank a little more into the mire of this uncomfortable and now scary feeling. This drug had not only flooded my whole existence; it had burst the banks of my consciousness. I was deeply regretting popping this pill, and sure I was now sledging, awaiting the onset of the coma-like vegetative state; petrified because I knew it was coming and there was nothing anyone could do about it. The fear and anxiety had now gripped me by the throat. It was strangling, asphyxiation was setting in, and I couldn't take a full breath. I had become icy cold, yet the sweat was dripping off me. As I manoeuvred my way towards the light, the clubbers stepped in front of me like vampires sent by their dark master,

MC Cosmic's dark hell-army, raining down on my path to freedom. These demons didn't want me to reach the light ahead of me. The light usually meant death, as in the film "Poltergeist." I could see shards of light over people's shoulders and through the gaps between their limbs: its origin, the frame of the chillout door, my door of sanctification. Surely this would lead to my salvation from this impending death fall? I had now arrived, wondering if death awaited me on the other side. Regardless, I was intent on escaping and leaving the darkness behind, so I flew through it, now on the other side, finally in the light chasing shallow breaths, still with a beat in my chest. Was I safe?

A momentary wave of relief fell like a warm blanket shrouding my trembling corpse. The surroundings were light and bright, the music was not as loud, and I hadn't yet thrown off my mortal coil. The momentary relief was soon overshadowed; I was in a war zone surrounded by the fallout. Many like me were sledging and struggling; someone had just vomited. The fastest way to exorcise the demonic poison from one's soul before it digested completely. Had I reached the point of no return? I needed to sit down as my legs didn't want to carry me anymore. The only seat was the end space on a wall-secured bench in the furthest corner of the room. I needed to calm down and see whether I could get a grip of this chemical plague that I could feel crawling from inside to out all over my dying flesh. I was sure I had just experienced my first death rattle, fighting to cling onto every breath as it left my mouth, swallowing it back as if it was the only air available to sustain my life. Now head in my hands, elbows on my knees, I felt like death. "WHAT HAVE I DONE," I thought? I actually shouted it out loud, which alerted everyone who was now staring. I needed a friend, but I knew nobody. I felt like I had ripped my heart out of my chest for safekeeping, staring at it in my hands, asking it to save me. I didn't want to travel any further down this road to hades, the highway to hell, begging the loudness of that electronic music to stop hurting my ears. I couldn't think clearly; like a banshee, it was shrieking, and the bass was thumping me into my grave with every beat. The death toll of the bass was intent on finding me, searching the room, pursuing my soul up through the wooden bench I was sat on, vibrating under its control and into my body, up to my spine and into my brain... GET OUT!

A momentary release: the bass dropped, which felt like silence as one choon ended and the next one was mixed in. The soft electronic sound of a pulsating oscillating organ was familiar, then the mid-range, "I know this song," here's the bass I used to love, then came the words, "Way in my brain." "I LOVE THIS CHOON!" suddenly, my whole body came to life. A chemical defibrillator had exploded in my chest; electricity was now coursing through my body. I was being resuscitated, reborn, and reformed. Had I been hit by lightning, every hair on my body now stood on end, goosebumps, even under my fingernails. All of me was rushing, elated; I was euphoric, I had never felt like this before, tears of joy, this is sooooooo good, and I was sooooo overwhelmed.

Had I just been pulled up out of a grave, now on my way back to the welcoming darkness of the dancefloor compelled by the urge to merge. MC Cosmic now in full chime, this time raising my mood, the music was penetrating every cell in my body, every atom was fizzing. The bass was caressing my skin, I was inside and outside the music at the same time, it had become a fluid medium of pure unadulterated bliss, which now immersed every fibre of my being soaking up and in every millisecond of this moment. The sound of the hypnotic beat had become three-dimensional. I could feel it on the outside of my skin, inside my soul and like the song declared 'WAY IN MY BRAIN'. Invisible fingertips were tantalizing the back of my neck, my whole body shimmered and quivered. The entire surface of my flesh felt like it had been turned into an ear, it was sensory transfiguration, no more did I want to be alone, like tribal consciousness, empathy shades into the telepathic, now lost in music hugging strangers, acknowledging others from afar, every thought of fear and dread like my spine had dissolved, not an ounce of anxiety, I was quite simply and utterly 'Loved Up' set free from my previous coffin like state, the deliverance placebo this choon by SL2. I journeyed back to find my friends huddled around the edge of the dance floor. It was emotional, brotherly love in its purest form. We had never hugged each other like this before, in fact we had never hugged each other at all. I didn't just feel more alive than ever before, as promised, I felt like I was now standing outside myself, my old self, the one that needed to die. I felt like the Phoenix rising from the ashes, escaping that fleshy disposition of sin, pain and hurt, stress and dread. Set free, I had stepped out of my dead bones and empty flesh. I was in love with the whole wide world and I just wanted to dance, which is exactly what I did for 4 hours straight.

Of course, there were some physical side effects, which like speed included dry mouth, grinding of teeth, excessive intake of air and face pulling. E had the opposite effect of a hangover. The afterglow ensured the following 24 hours were soothingly blissful. The major repercussion of doing the drug was the comedown a few days later, I felt fatigued. What I had just gone through and come out of was tantamount to an emotional burnout, experiencing occasional mood swings between relation and desolation, that felt comparable to heartbreak, so I had to do it again, and again. I had been on an emotional spree. I could not wait to see what the next new tablet in circulation would be and what that trip would be like, because it was always different. There were many brands and experiences of E distinguished by their colouring and tiny pictograms stamped into the tablet including, Pink Pigs, New Yorkers, Adam and Eves, Dennis the menace's, Rhubarb and Custards, Love hearts, Flatliners, Disco Biscuits and I am sure there's many more, but the most popular of all was the Dove. However, my favourite was a Snowball. They were shaped like a ball of snow, super powerful and I only needed half. My all-time favourite choon by Ramirez called 'Hablando', YouTube it, was licking the airwaves of the club. I was standing by the biggest speaker snowballed in the darkest corner of this warehouse sinking into this bed of bass, the air pressure of the sound being pumped out of the dark black cone and tweeter, the cushion of sound pressure keeping me upright preventing me from falling into this megaphone of pure delight. My eyes rolled up into the back of my head, the sound emanating through my whole existence, into the depths of my mind, heart and soul taking me to a place of absolute arrival, pulsating vibrating joy, a musical grenade blowing up pain and hurt out of existence by the power and sound of the psychedelic multi coloured drug induced coma. It was as if I was intravenously kept alive by the trance harmonic beat of this absolute CHOOOONNNN!!! Unsafely lost in music, out of my mind, inside my soul, born for a time like this in the exact place and moment I was I mistakenly thought I was meant to be. Hands in the air worship the DJ, I thought I had been so found, little did I know then I was more lost than lost can be.

Chapter 27

All that glitters is not gold

I wasn't sure if this chemical had opened up a hurt locker. Comfortably numb pain had been normal for so long that I didn't know it existed. Exposed when set free by the drug-induced high, it was more acutely felt in the comedown. That said, I didn't feel like I had worked through five months of emotional blockages in five hours. I'd spent ten years of my life in the cult. Although I had not been emotionally and physiologically disarmed, I was certainly more vulnerable, at least to the once comfortably numb pain of rejection and loss I suffered, leaving all my cult friends and wider family behind. A life once lived, wiped out instantly, non-transferable, left with the position of trying to catch up, but that which could not be caught. I had to rediscover ten years of my life; the most formative years occupied in the cult.

From eleven years of age, I was preoccupied with trying to recover and become a non-cult member. Now 20 years of age, I was left wondering why I had become so rebellious. Was it in protest to the rules that once controlled me? Now the laws of the land, the rules of the world, could not control me. A once very sheltered life, now a stark contrast to the life I lived. Had I really left that ten-year-old boy behind? Was I actually reborn into this brave new world, another version of me, or just tolerating it, papering over the cracks, living for the moment, so I didn't have to think too hard about the past? I had my Dad taken away from me twice. He was sent to a bedsit as a leper, then to jail. As a kid I saw too many dead bodies of people who were not family. I experienced the deaths of my grandparents, whose funerals I couldn't attend, and I never grieved. It was as if they never existed. Did I grieve the life I had left behind in the cult? Every friend, cousin, or similar, I was dead to; did they grieve me? Did all that really happen to me? It felt like it happened to someone else.

Was I clinging on to life, not sure which life was the right one, pre or post-cult, trying to move forward with one foot stuck in the past, the other stepping into the unknown? If I was Godless, why did I have a massive guilt complex, or was it simply indoctrination still calling the tune to some of the life decisions I tried to make? For eighteen years of my life, I lived clean. It took two short years to destroy it. Was it the best two years of my life because of excessive drug abuse? Was it really just the pursuit of self-seeking hedonism, or simply self-soothing in the absence of absolutely no therapy, support, or assistance to readjust from that life I left behind? Did I need to grieve the loss of ten years of my life? Were these the emotional blockages I was meant to be working through, which those Ecstasy therapists claimed could be fast-tracked, or was this the revelation of pain, that I now used drugs to numb, when before, normality was the safety net of my ignorant bliss? I never really felt blissful until I took E. Was I a little boy lost simply playing the victim and using this to excuse my bad, often inappropriate behaviour, drug use and abuse, and the reason I ultimately went to jail? The telling of that event is still to come…

It's hard to reconcile that for eighteen years, I was effectively strait-laced and teetotal. I had never been in trouble with the police, yet after two years, I was behind bars. The very thing I thought I was escaping from was the only place I could function with any degree of normality. Despite the attraction of TV, music, etc., this new world at best had a novelty value only, and at worst exposed me to a world I never knew, to which I should have spent my first ten years acclimatising. I just wasn't prepared. Everything I saw, I believed. My sponge-like messed-up head soaked up the bad as truth, and it was going to happen to me, so I lived out of fear.

Did drugs set me free from fear or expose it as no longer normal? Was it just simply the release I craved, even if for one night only as my mind was chemically exorcised of all its demons? Was one night of bliss worth the next six days, clinging on in pursuit of the weekend so I could be saved again? Was I saved or seeking comfort in a thickly veiled momentary counterfeit heaven? I didn't know.

I soon realised that all that glitters is not actually gold, and not everything that felt precious and true turns out to be so. Drugs were not the answer.

Imagine your life as a graph; your normal is a straight horizontal line. When you experience the high of, say, Ecstasy, the line on the graph is almost vertical, and peaks until it retreats as the drugs wear off and creates the shape of a mountain. But the line doesn't arrive back in the same place you were before the high. You go lower than the normal straight horizontal line that was once your life. The line and graph now look more like a valley, an open wound exposing all your baggage, pain and hurt you tried to forget and thought you had forgotten. The highs get fewer, but the valleys become much deeper until the buzz is no more, and you use drugs to simply survive. Cannabis, now my pacifier to get me to the weekend so E could obliterate all the pain again, became the medicine helping me deal with the mundane day-to-day life. Before drugs, I was comfortable drinking in secret in my bedroom. All weed did was replace the Southern Comfort, but now I knew why I needed to self-soothe. Beforehand, it was an innate desire to feel okay and manage my emotions. Normal was no longer interesting. It never was, but now I knew this more acutely, so I enjoyed being out of my mind, off my head. The past needed deadening, as it had not been dealt with psychologically. I did hide a lot of emotions; if you asked anybody who knew me then, they would never have known. I had cultivated the art of hiding in plain sight. It began in senior school, later covered up by humour, and I lived just enough to never be alone with my thoughts too long.

Chapter 28

Vicki from the block

Let me interject to tell you about my Vicki, who is now my wife. Most days, we would hang out in the canteen at college. On this particular and very special day, I was sat with Shotgun Lee. We didn't know each other then, but Vicki was standing with her back to me at the servery getting lunch. I always had a thing for brunettes, and straight away I spotted her luscious curly brown hair, like a lion's mane down her back. She was wrapped in a figure-hugging black leather three-quarter coat and rose-patterned blue Jeans, with black Bronx boots. I knew right away, even before she turned to face me, she was… a right bit of me. I had only seen the back of her and I knew she was right. When she did turn, I was hooked. She was cute, but sexy with olive skin, part Iranian. Ordinarily, I had been intent on doing drugs and partying with the lads and would usually avoid romantic connections. This time, I wanted to know this girl, I wanted to take her out, and moreover, this was the first time I had felt drawn to another since my first real relationship 3 years prior. I knew her friend Kate: she lived opposite my house, so naturally, our paths would cross and Vicki was soon part of our circle of college friends. I was smitten, but I could not muster up the confidence to approach her romantically for some time. At least, we were now talking to each other.

This wasn't normal to me, but I couldn't suppress what I felt, caught up in this fresh spellbinding breath of love-filled air, trained in the art of

ensuring what I was feeling on the inside was not manifesting on the
out. Had it been, I was sure she would have gone. I didn't even give
her the eyes properly; you know when you want someone to know you
fancy them and you stare until they notice and quickly look away, but
too late so you can get caught on purpose. I just stirred, and when I
wasn't stirring, I wouldn't shut up, trying to be relatable and cool, but
fearing the opposite. I had just met this girl, and usually, I was only
this open with the opposite sex under the influence of drugs or drink.
The Kingsman pub was on the way home for Vicki, and so I plucked
up the courage to ask if she would like to stop by. I was testing the lie
of the land. She agreed. Is right! There were six of us, and when we
arrived I was now sitting next to her, getting to know her. Accidentally
on purpose, I brushed my leg up against hers, leaving it there to see if
she pulled away. She didn't. Is right! I had my Walkman on, and she
was now sharing my headphones, one earphone in her ear the other
in mine, listening to songs we loved. Her favourite was mine, a techno
song called, 'Here's Johnny, bowooochibow'. She was into techno, went
to the same clubs as I, and now we were lost in each other's company,
this bubble of intimacy. We were soon pulled out of it when the others
started sniggering because they could see what we could feel, we were
falling for each other.

I left with Vicki, and plucked up the courage to ask if she would come
out on Friday; we were going to The State nightclub. Vicki thought
it unlikely as she may be babysitting, interestingly, Gary Ablett's kids,
what a coincidence! I wonder whether the kids are called Charlie and
Billy. Was this a knock-back or a sign? But Shotgun Lee and Kate
had colluded and become our matchmakers, to do what Vicki and I
couldn't. He was now walking with Vicki and I was with Kate. It was
soon settled: unbeknown to me The Shotgun was now telling Vicki
exactly how I felt, and Kate was telling me exactly how Vicki felt. It was
a match, I was buzzing. Vicki couldn't make the Friday night out, but
we would meet up the following Sunday. After the evening together,
made uniquely all the more memorable when she fell and ripped her

leather pants, (then did her best to make it look like it hadn't happened in the hope I didn't seen her - for the sake of love, I pretended I hadn't noticed), she and I kissed for the first time.

Vicki well and truly won every beat of my heart, then and thereafter. Victoria was the victor. Twenty eight years later, we are now married and blessed with 3 beautiful daughters.

Chapter 29

Mr Big

We can all pinpoint a time or person in our lives, an influence, a crossroads, which led us down a certain path. A decision we wished we could go back and change, or nostalgically re-live, thankful as that choice set in motion who, and what we became, instrumental in forming everything that is good in and about our lives, or wishful thinking, if only we could go back and change what set in motion who, and what we became. When life goes well or we survive against the odds some say, "someone up there is looking out for me." What do we say when things turn out bad? One other very significant new friend landed smack bang in the middle of a significant crisis in my life. I was so fed up with my body and about to buy steroids. Dave the marine was a bodybuilder. Several months before meeting The Marine I had started going to the gym, in fact I was taking weight gain supplements, but nothing substantial was happening. Any weight gained I soon burnt off taking drugs and dancing the night away. I said to The Marine, "how did you get that big," initially he wasn't forthcoming, but when I told him I was thinking of taking steroids The Marine introduced me to his best mate Steve 'The Fox' who was even bigger than him, and interestingly was one of my partners in crime. He was a red head, hence the name The Fox.

These meatheads had taken me to their gym, so I was now training properly. This was the choice gym for all the major gangsters in the south of Liverpool, those that didn't want to kill each other. The

Fox and The Marine were known so I was accepted within these underworld circles quite quickly. Soon, I started injecting steroids, I had put on three stone of muscle. I had stretch marks and looked like an absolute Adonis.

I was spending more time with these two new friends who were mixing with Liverpool's underworld. Mr Big trained in the gym we started going to. He invited us to the nightclub he held the door at and gave us a walkover, otherwise known as a free pass. That night, we saw him, and another drag a drug dealer kicking and screaming into the toilets. They taxed him, which meant they had taken all his drugs rouged him up, and then exited him from the club. The 50 or so ecstasy tablets taxed were passed to us. We necked several and agreed to sell the rest on the basis our mate on the door 'Mr Big' got half the sale proceeds. They sold like hot cakes in less than 30 minutes and we made £500, the only problem, word got around the club we were selling Gary's. We soon realised we could have sold another 500 just as quick. Whilst this was exciting, unfortunately it was the wrong place at the wrong time with the wrong people. On this very night, a simple night out with the lads doing what we loved opened a door that I could not close. This unsuspecting night ushered in my unwholesome hellish descent into Liverpool's underworld as a participant, this was the night I became an accidental gangster.

We were invited to an evening with Mr Big. He wanted to discuss how we turned 50 tablets into £500 in less than 30 minutes, could we replicate that night, but with more tablets. Were we interested? Hell yeah, was the collective response from this famous five, The Fox, The Shotgun, The Bumper, Hiawatha and me. The offer, Mr Big would supply the drugs, protection and we would have full control of the club, all he wanted was 50% of the sale proceeds. This club was the No.1 club in Liverpool and was fast becoming the No.1 club in the country so we would have the rich pickings of 2,000 clubbers every Saturday night.

Why did we accept Mr Bigs offer without a second thought? We didn't even sleep on it. Did we really know what we were getting into, or were we blinded by the thrill and enhanced reputation? The deception, it didn't even feel like we were breaking the law. We weren't hanging around in the shadows, or on a street corner. Not only had we dealt a Class A drug that first night, we were now conspiring to do the same. Possession threatened a prison term of 5 years, actual supply 7 years (sold as a one off) and 10 years for what we were about to do, sell E again, in the eyes of the law it's called conspiracy! Previously, I had been so cautious.

What had made me become so indifferent, if not passive to these consequences? What fuelled this complete ignorance of risk and false sense of security? First off, taking drugs had become normal, I was doing it every day, and Mr Big's business proposal came with fringe benefits, we would have exclusivity over the club to sell with the full protection of the door. Furthermore, we would not be carrying drugs 24/7. We would effectively take delivery the same day we sold them in the club, and leave drug free, cash rich. This seemed an absolute no brainer and almost risk free. Furthermore, it was not like selling heroin to addicts who had just robbed whoever to get a fix. Ecstasy was not addictive, and we were selling to the middle class, professionals, posh people, rich students. In this club there were no Berghaus ninjas, there was a strict dress code and at £15 it was the most expensive club in Liverpool to gain entry. If there had been any reticence or resistance, the deal was ultimately sealed when we realised this was a promotion and being a drug dealer carried a certain amount of underworld prestige within the circles we mixed with. We were not only firmed up, but we were made men.

As a made man, in the space of 3 years I had gone from a malnourished, morose, insecure boy struggling to break puberty with hygiene problems, afraid of my own shadow, to an utter specimen of a man, with hair like a rock star, money to burn, dressed to impress, with a killer reputation, feared because of who I knew. This was the best I had ever felt, of course superficial, because deep inside nothing had really changed, although I didn't have time to think about that boy that was once me. However, for this season of my life I forgot the past and revelled in the present, I was on top of the world, defined by my circumstances. I was relevant, popular, and part of something much bigger than I could have ever imagined. My ego was being fuelled like no other time before, in fact, finally I had an ego. The way I felt, I would have almost said yes to Mr Big and dealt his drugs for free, the fringe benefits were too attractive. In all honesty, on that night Mr Big made that offer, I said yes without absolutely no thought of the consequences. I was sure whatever the risk, it would not happen to me. Famous last words. I was sworn in, it was official, I was a drug dealer, a significant cog in Mr Bigs drug dealing machine. The following Saturday would be the night this enterprise would be launched, it had arrived, but was I ready!?

Chapter 30

I am a drug dealer!

The Fox would make the pickup and we would share 500 tablets, they were Doves. 200 for The Shotgun and The Fox, 300 for The Bumper, Hiawatha and me. Effectively 100 Gary's each. It was decided we three would take the big room. On this particular Saturday we met in The Fox's house and left with our 300 pills. I was the carrier and dedicated promoter, Hiawatha would take the money, The Bumper would supply the tablet to the customer. It was agreed when we arrived at the club I would be positioned outside the toilet where I could generate custom and point them to Hiawatha and The Bumper nearby. When The Bumper ran out, I would release another 50 tablets from my bikini. I am going to be completely straight with you, at this point I was wearing a pair of my sister's bikini knickers, they were lime green with assorted imprints of tropical fruit. They were stretched tight to my midriff, too tight to unload my meat and veg into, but loose enough that it could hold the tablets securely, with my normal underwear over the top. I didn't care what I was wearing, because it meant I had no drugs in my pockets. If I was stopped and searched, they would find nothing unless I was undressed.

Walking the streets with a drug pouch, which had a street value of £5,000, I could not risk losing my consignment. This scared me more than the police finding out, because if I lost the drugs I was answerable to Mr Big for £5,000 big ones I didn't have. Whilst our friendship had been apparent, now it was very much business only, and I didn't want to get kneecapped for losing his gear. What was usually a typical A to B journey to the nightclub, had become perilous in the extreme, at least in my mind. Instantly, it became very real for the first time. I don't know what scared me more, being arrested, losing them or being taxed by another firm on the way to the club. In this moment all infatuation with my newfound status as a connected protected gangster dissipated. I realised I had been swept along and away in the inertia of that first night, and then blinded by the bright lights of gangster hood. I didn't really give any thought to the reality this moment was now alarmingly alerting me to. I was bricking it, and the only thing stopping what was threatening to leave my arsehole was the 300 pills that were lodged between my hoop and ball bag in my sister's bikini. I tried to take my mind off this illegal parcel, but every step I made the edge of the bag would nip my scrotum and whilst it was not sharp enough to hurt, it meant I had absolutely no chance of forgetting what was nestling in my undercarriage, which was also useful, as every time one of my nuts was elbowed by this bag I knew it was still there and hadn't fallen out of my trouser leg.

I had entered The Fox's house as calm as a Hindu cow, and left like McVicar, now glancing over my shoulder long enough I was still able to walk in a straight line, nearly putting my neck out, enough that I had 360° eyeballs on my surrounding subjects, wondering if the parked car was an undercover cop, was that really a pizza delivery man, sure that dog walker was following me, or was there a crew firmed up waiting to pull me into the alley and tax me. This was not how I imagined things would be when we conspired around that table in the pub. I had never been so aware of my surroundings, which was heightened by my overactive imagination. I was drowning in thoughts of the very real consequences I previously disregarded. Have you ever been in a public space aware of the serious possibility should the stars align, at least for the police, you were going down for 10 years, it's terrifying. I did not want to do anymore, what I was about to do, stuck between a rock and a hard place. The rock, it was too late I had the pills on my person in public, the hard place, Mr Big wanted a return on his investment. I also now knew too much, if I got arrested, like in the films, the one being played out across the screen of my mind, would my family be persecuted to stop me informing. The way I was feeling I may as well have been handcuffed already on my way to jail, trapped again. I was all in and now didn't want to be. Selling the drugs this night was the only way I could get rid of them, at least without ending up in the river Mersey wearing a pair of concrete boots.

We arrived at the club. I was doing my best to remain calm, surrounded by the management, and the doormen, although covertly they knew who I was, I still had to be patted down for effect. Regardless, they weren't paid enough to run their fingers along the underside of my nut sack or lift it up and rummage behind it. In any event they didn't care if I was carrying a machine gun they just needed to go through the motions for the benefit of the management. We confirmed our names, the ones we made up, and we were in. Once in the club, Mr big strolled passed, winked and out the side of his mouth said, "meet me in the toilets." I followed him into the first empty cubicle. "Take these," he said. More drugs, no I thought, which included a load of what we thought was speed, a dealer had been taxed and launched, this was his gear. I say we thought, we later took this suspicious powder and never slept for two days, wired, uncontrollably twitching and chewing our tongues, seeing things that weren't there. As soon as Mr Big left the toilets, I gave it two minutes then also left, we could not be seen colluding.

I took up my position outside the toilet. It was my turn to spit out, "ya after any Gary's." Straight off the bat the first person said "yes," then another, they kept coming. As quickly as they arrived, I directed them to Hiawatha and The Bumper. Word soon spread I was the tablet man. I was not sure this was a good thing. I craved popularity, but not like this. Incredibly, within an hour we had sold out. No sooner had this conveyor belt of supply kicked in, we realised how seamless and quick it was to effectively raise close to £5,000 in little over an hour. Not only was this a thrill, we were celebrated by those that we sold to, they would find us to thank us for the buzz they were now on. How messed up was this! All concern about doing this again had dissipated. Whilst I don't endorse what I did, it was addictive, certainly exciting, and I had never seen so much money in my life, nor had I been so popular amongst so many strangers. It was the easiest thing I had ever done; with the greatest reward and I now thought the least risk. Again, the only problem, we didn't have enough tablets, but that would change as demand increased, so did supply and I recall on one night, which was an all-nighter 1,000 tablets sold as quick as we could get them out of my sisters' bikini. By this time, we were well established in the club and any thought of being caught was lost on how easy it was and the adrenaline fuelled buzz. That was until I got that call, we had a meet, I had to be there! We were meeting a rival firm, one of the most feared firms in Liverpool, they wanted to take over the door and take our business off us, this is how it played out.

Chapter 31

Sawn off shotgun!

I was partying most nights, certainly on drugs of one kind or another every day of the week. I had added ketamine to my growing lists of experiences, horse tranquiliser, really!!! It was getting out of hand. Sunday, we met up as a firm. Monday we would be clubbing. Tuesday and Wednesday would be our chill out days, but we would be smoking copious amounts of weed. Thursday we would go to the Buzz Club, Friday the Drome. When I wasn't in the club snorting or swallowing, or at home smoking drugs we were in the gym training and injecting drugs. What a terrible life, it was 100 mph and it was heading in one direction, although I didn't know it. I had the very thing I thought I wanted. I had little time or desire to think about the past or any space in my mind for it, because most of the time I was under the influence of one drug or another, popping E like smarties. I knew it was beginning to go pear shaped when I started taking E in the middle of the day and started using cocaine. Cocaine was not a high demand drug at the time, but it was the next thing I had not done and my 21st birthday seemed a fitting occasion. We were going to The State. I loved the buzz of doing a bit of beak, as we called it back then, beak referenced the nose, others called it bugle as it was an instrument you had to blow by sucking up the air through your nose, the same I was about to do with this powder. I didn't like how it numbed the top of my nostrils. Nor did I take to the bitter taste in the back of my throat, and it would make my face tingle. At first it felt like it gave me unlimited energy and confidence, but it didn't last. It was twice the price of one ecstasy tablet that did last, and when taken together lessened the buzz of E. That night I had to do more E. That night I was off my cake, a cocktail of Charlie and Gary's, plus I had also injected steroids earlier in the day, looking back this was simply obscene. Yes, I had a night to remember, although I can only recall it in part, this time I wasn't dancing, I was told my eyes had rolled up into the back of my head, and for a period I needed to be supervised. Yes, I had taken too much, more than my body could handle, but I paid for it physically. I didn't sleep properly for a week.

What goes up had to come down. Pumping all sorts of chemicals into my body every day started to leave its mark. I had started to break out in horrific acne, particularly when I was on a heavy course of steroids, I later needed prescribed steroids to get rid of the acne illegal steroids caused. When the club started doing all-nighters on Fridays, basically 10pm to 6am the following day, I was working Friday and Saturday again. This had become a business where Mr Big was intent on making as much money as possible with us taking most of the risk. The lifestyle really started to change when we learnt that it had gone off outside BIG TIME, a major gangster firm had come to take over the door from our firm. It was at this point the lifestyle I had turned in on me. I became a face in a rival firm, which meant I had enemies who were serious gangsters, so I was a target. I now needed the protection of the gang, and the novelty of selling drugs was wearing thin, so this was the straw that broke the camel's back. I didn't want to do it anymore, the excitement had been replaced by fear, plus working Friday and Saturday nights I was partying less, nor could I leave because we were now in a rivalry with another Liverpool firm and of course I knew too much. In fact, a meet had been arranged with this other firm, a straightener, last man standing would take the business. Usually the weapon of choice was our fists, not on this night, I got the shock of my life.

I was told to be on standby, we were going mob handed to meet this other firm. I got the call around about 4 pm on that Sunday, the one

I hoped would never come. I had to be at a designated location near our meet to strategize. Every ounce of me wanted to stay at home, run away, but I couldn't for two reasons. First off, this rival firm were serious gangsters and not to be messed with. Around this time, they shunned two of their soldiers, but not without first opening them up dragging a blade down the side of their cheek so the scar would stay for life. If they did this to their own, what would they do to me? Secondly, I needed the protection of my firm against my firm. To not turn up would label me a shit bag. I would be cast out, and in my mind possibly hurt to scare me into secrecy, but I had no choice, so reluctantly I had to meet up with the gang. There was no way out. On my way to our strategy meeting I was plotting my own escape plan, when it kicked off I would be in eye shot, but I would do my best to avoid the frontline, with an easy escape route from the periphery if it got too much.

Mr Big special reserves were now sat around the table of a pub near our final destination, it was a carvery in an affluent suburb of Liverpool, families were eating their Sunday roasts. Mr Big had not yet turned up. The Bumper sat next to me was fidgeting messing with his pockets. I said, "what's up with you," he said, "these keep digging into me." I said, "what?". "These shotgun shells!" Now confused I said, "what have you got them for?" The Bumper casually pointed to Shotgun Lee and said, "to put in that," as Shotgun Lee flashed me an eyeful of what he was carrying, it was a sawn off. This was not only the first time I learnt we were going in armed; this was the first time I had ever seen a real gun. It then dawned on me how serious this was. I wanted to run and never stop, and no sooner had this negotiation in my head began, "should I stay, or should I go," Mr Big walked in. Too late, I wasn't going anywhere. I was now being ushered into to the nightclub where we would await our encounter with the rival firm. After about an hour we knew it was on, as they were now in the club looking for us. No sooner had we laid eyes on each other the place erupted.

I was led to believe the back of the club was where it was going to take place, so naturally, despite my original intention to remain, but at arm's length, I was heading in the other direction, as were those who were just socialising, who now knew this was no place to be at this moment. It was like a fire drill, I was so scared running that fast I fell down the outside staircase I was using to escape this scene, the opposite direction from where I thought it was going off. I got it so wrong; it was taking place in the front of the club. How did I know, when I finally managed to gather myself after surviving the external staircase stunt roll, I was now standing dead centre in the middle of this meet, you couldn't have scripted it better, Mr Big one side, the Head of the other firm the other, surrounded by their firm now pulling guns out the back of their cars. Out of the corner of my eye I could see The Shotgun and The Bumper loading up our piece, the reality, it was a complete do it yourself job if this weapon went off everybody was getting it. Mr Big and the other head now spitting hate at each other, I felt like the referee in the ring ready to start overseeing a world title fight waiting for the bell to ring so Armageddon could commence. Out of nowhere another head, a gangster who had no skin in the game, parted the crowd and started talking these two guys down. This guy carried some authority and stepped into the middle of this shit storm. "There's too many eyes, too many witnesses, this has to stop right now," I couldn't agree more, although I didn't say it out loud. No sooner had this truth been spoken the signal was given and the guns disappeared, you could hear the car boot doors closing one after the other, and everybody backed off. Inside I breathed the biggest sigh of relief, outside I was pretending I was ready for action. What was bizarre, we headed back to a safe house with these gangsters some of them serious heads who couldn't wait to shake my hand, "you were there lad, no fear, ultimate respect," little did they know, I was quite the opposite, the irony, I was actually trying to escape running away from the scene, I thought it was in the other direction, the only bullets I was firing were out of my arse hole, but one after another I was being lifted high by these serious men.

This was another promotion, but one I didn't want. It was now apparent; at least in my mind, my life was in danger and I needed to escape this world but was now deeper in than I had ever been, trapped again, the biggest accidental gangster you could imagine. However, what I didn't realise, circumstances were about to effectively deal me a get out of jail card. When I sold to two clubbers, as regrettable as this was, they gave me a route out, the one I wanted when I realised, I was solely responsible for what happened. Whilst the clubbers survived, the police were involved, my customers were able to describe me in detail. I was told to stay away from the club, which coincidentally gave me the chance to safely leave this drug ring and save face whilst keeping the firm's protection. That said paranoia kicked in, I was left wondering if I had become public enemy No.1, now on the police's radar, what if I was caught off guard by the rival firm I had so unceremoniously introduced myself to first-hand, that night when I fell down the stairs. I wasn't sure if I had escaped, or if I was staving off the inevitable. Did I need to go into hiding or just get back to normal life.

I didn't feel safe, and fear had gripped me by the throat. What I thought had delivered me from the pain of my past had quite literally created a hellish existence. Was this another sign sent from God to save me from the destination 'fate' was so hell-bent on sending me to? I was so close to escaping once and for all; however, the curse of the cult came back to haunt me one more time. Did I have a choice? I was going to be made homeless, so I was drawn back into this world and repositioned back on my path, toward the total destruction of my life

Chapter 32

The curse of the cult

Mum had received a very distressing letter. She needed me to accompany her to see a solicitor to discuss its contents. This was a letter like numerous others before, but this time she got to it before Dad could conceal it. The solicitor was a friend of Mum's, agreed to assist and confirmed in no uncertain terms the loan taken out in 1982 to reimburse the cult, 12 years later had escalated to £105,000, now greater than the value of the house. This meant the bank was going to file a repossession order with the courts to evict us from our home. Of course, it came as no great surprise, but the amount we owed did, and shook us to the core. Why was it so much? Even if Dad was employable, any chance of paying the loan back was taken from him when he was sent to jail, despite paying the cult back before the authorities were made aware. All the equity in the house was eroded. Ultimately, it was the cult that subjected us to those extreme circumstances. They effectively left Dad up shit creek without a paddle, sending him out into a strange world, jobless, unskilled, uneducated, and without a reference. Actually, by pursuing him through the courts, they gave him the worst reference of all, a criminal record. My first and quite natural thought was: where are we going to live? I needed to raise money for a rent deposit and rent, plus the cost of moving. Just when I thought I had escaped, I was dragged back into crime and the underworld to pay for it all. The risk was surely worth it, as the alternative, homelessness, wasn't. What I couldn't come to terms with was the fact that the cult was still messing with our lives all this time on.

I contacted Mr Big and asked if I could return, not sure if he'd let me. As some time had passed, he agreed I could, although, I would have to wear a disguise. We settled on a bandanna, and I had to wear my glasses. I looked like a clever traveller, or at the very least a short-sighted bull-fighter. The need to raise money fast far outweighed the risk of looking like an utter melt, or of the threat of jail and being catapulted back into the centre of that turf war I thought I left behind.

I was soon back dealing again, under my new guise 'Benny Blanco' from the caravan site. As soon as the money was rolling in again, oblivion descended like a smog. It had become about my little six inches of grass yet again, no thought to beyond the risk, skulduggery, and dangers that lay ahead. Accordingly, a new course of steroids was purchased. This time, I would hit the gear hard. I wanted to get to 15 stone, with 18-inch arms. Whilst I soon realised I did miss the buzz of dealing and the infamy that came with it, now I was dealing solely out of necessity. When I had enough money, I had decided I was getting out once and for all.

The crew I had re-joined had widened their criminal network. As always, we went back to one party or another, but now they were much shadier, as were some of the people we were associating with. Let me introduce The Hammer, when leaving the club, we were in a Porsche Carrera, owned by the son of the busiest ice cream van operator in Liverpool, we had a lot of rich clingons, which for the most part we humoured, why wouldn't we when we were chauffeured around in cars like this. However, we could not get through the crowd. The Hammer was known as The Hammer because he always carried a hammer and would use it gratuitously as and when the mood took him. Because we couldn't get through this crowd, out it came, and the unsuspecting crowd were now getting it. The last time I saw a crowd part and run this quickly I was in first place fleeing from the rival firm on that Sunday night of that meet. I can also recall a story when the boss of this firm at a party lost his rag and put a pair of scissors into the side of the unsuspecting victims face. WHAT HAD I GOT MYSELF INVOLVED IN!!!

Around this time Hiawatha was close to a girl in the club. She had asked if he could meet her to provide tablets outside the club, interestingly in the same boozer several weeks before we were sat around the unsuspecting carvery eating families preparing our sawn-off shotgun for war. Selling drugs outside of the club was something ordinarily we would not do. However, it was me who ended up being sent to meet this girl and do the deal. She never turned up and we never saw her again. This was a set up, we later learned her brother was a police officer. This was an attempt to lure us out of the club to break the law so the police could thicken their file on us. How I didn't suspect this was a set up at the time I don't know but it was certainly yet another a sign to turn from what I was doing and avoid the path I was on.

Paranoia had started to take hold, ramped up like never before when The Bumper and I were sat off with this other head. He was a Heroin dealer. He had just got a message on his pager and learnt that the police had been sniffing around his car, so this guy was hot-tailing out of the party we were in, back to his house. Now, on his way back with The Bumper in the front seat magically balancing a large mirror with a load of uncut heroin on it, The Hammer drove around the streets of Liverpool trying to avoid the police. There was no time to wrap it or pour it into a bag. I don't know what was scarier, losing the gear off the side of the mirror all over his car, or being caught by the police who **weren't** in pursuit. When something like this happens, fear spreads like a virus and paranoia sets in. If the police were on to this smack dealer, then they were on to us. It was our turn to hot-tail it out of this party. The Bumper had been hiding the sawn-off shotgun in his mum's attic, and I now had all the shotgun shells. We were en route to the field at the back of our house. The sun was rising and the sparrows tweeting as we were unloading all our paraphernalia under the Cockies hut, the place I grew up then as an innocent kid. Glancing for a moment across at my favourite hiding place when we used to play hide-n-seek, I realised how unrecognisable my life had become. Why didn't I just stop right there and then? It transpired that this was the last warning I ever got.

My date with destiny was now set and I was racing headlong into the middle of this nightmare with my name on it.

March the 12th 1994 and the day had finally arrived. The family were all awoken by heavy knocking on our front door. It was early and not too long after 8 am. It was an enforcement officer with the bailiffs. We were getting evicted! Did we really believe they wouldn't follow through on that death note to evict? Why were we still there? We had half an hour to pack up any essentials and leave our home forever. We had been lulled into a false sense of security as the house was not repossessed 30 days later as expected, because the bank had found a buyer, so it was now the new purchaser who was effectively kicking us out. Thankfully, I was able to live with The Bumper temporarily. Friends came to the aid of the rest of my family, but we were separated, a fractured family yet again, and my Dad was gone for the third time. For what good the last 12 years had done, we may as well have been back in the cult. Not only had IT excommunicated Dad, but now his only surviving family, us, shunned him. How utterly harrowing, even if it was self-imposed. It was as if the last 12 years did not happen, removed from his home by the cult now blamed by his family for losing their home because of the cult. He had absolutely no one. The irony was sickening. The cult, in particular Dad's nemesis, had finally got his way, but this time it was at the cost of our family being made homeless.

One particular evening I'd spent it with Vicki and upon returning to The Bumper's place, he was out with Hiawatha, which I knew could turn into an all-nighter. I didn't have a key and The Bumper's mum was away, so I was locked out. Realising I could be here waiting for a long time, I decided to go home…to the house we had just been booted out of. It was the strangest feeling I ever did have, and it saddened me to the depths of my heart. In the dark of the night, only the streetlights to guide me shining through the windows, I broke in and climbed back into the same un-made bed that I was pulled out of the day the bailiffs came. Alone in the dark of the home I had grown up in, no longer a resident, I was now a trespasser in the place I celebrated Liverpool returning as champions, the place my Mum used to read countless illegal Famous Five books whilst she tickled the inside of my arm, the place I caught Dad leaving under cover of the night on the landing as he was heading back to his bedsit, the place I learned how to become me, the place I loved and lost. The echoes of my life there flooded my mind. However it didn't feel like home anymore. If I listened long enough I could hear my sister running across the landing to launch a paper ball at my head, the one I had just thrown at her, before running back to my room, and Dad catching her shouting us back to bed, or Dad shouting up the stairs at me to turn the music down, and me shouting back "it won't go any louder." I realised home is where your heart is, your heart is where your family is, those you love the most. That final night alone in my bed helped me deal with the fact I would never be able to live in this house again, or sleep in this bed another night, but at least I got the chance to formally say a final farewell. By the light of the early morning sun, I was able to reclaim many of my personal belongings, which I couldn't take when we were removed and I headed back to The Bumper's house.

When my Mum was given social housing status, fast-tracked by her friend Petrona, the elected councillor to the Labour Ward in Granby, Toxteth, we took the first thing we were offered, despite it being in one of the poorest areas in Liverpool. I moved in straight away with Mum. Dad was now back unsettled in that bedsit. Mum and I moved into our new home on the 31st of March 1994, my sister and brother would follow soon after. It was in one of the less desirable areas in Liverpool, although we would soon come to realise this was a community, unlike the one we left. People smiled at each other, strangers said hello to each other, and people seemed more welcoming and kind than the snobs we left behind. In fact, for the ten years my family spent in this home, we made some of the most memorable and fondest memories we ever did have, apart from the catastrophic one we were about to experience.

Interestingly, I now lived nearer to Liverpool city centre so the journey to the nightclub was a short one, I could walk it. This was also the area that provided several venues for a lot of parties we frequented and not too far from where The Fox lived, plus I had friends from the scene who lived nearby. I must refer to one particular guy. His name was Davo, he lived with his mum, loved his weed and nights out on E, lived for the weekend, but despite being the most sensible scall I ever did know, it seemed he had no future. That was until he met his significant other outside of his circle of destruction. He had fallen in love with an Irish girl and jumped at the chance to escape our world, one destined for jail, addiction, and premature death. He left and went to live in Ireland, where he got a job as a tyre fitter with a national brand who loved him that much he was featured on their advertisement across all the buses in Ireland. Whilst only a tyre fitter compared to what he left and where he was destined, by contrast, Davo had made it. That was until one Saturday night in his local chippy. He saw a kid getting battered outside and went to his aid; which was the last good thing he ever did, as he ended up taking a knife in the chest and died on the floor in front of the chippy. When he came back to Liverpool, the place he had escaped, he returned in a coffin.

Chapter 33

Arrested

Mum and I had been at our new house for two weeks. It was a Friday; the time was around 8.00 pm. Reluctantly, I said my goodbyes to Mum and left to go to the club as usual. I promised Mum I would not be back too late, as I didn't want to leave her on her own. Little did she know I would not return as promised. I didn't even return the following day, and when I finally did arrive home, she was not there and I was in handcuffs under the control of two police officers. On that Friday night, I was in my dedicated position in the club, doing the business, as usual, bandanna on, not a bull in sight or the chance of ever seeing one. The clock had just struck 9.30, the night was well underway, and tablets were getting sold left right and centre, at this rate I could be home before 12. I was down to my last fifty-six tablets. The lights went up and the club music came to a grinding halt. It was startling, but not as startling as what was about to happen to me.

Normally it's Friday 13th that's the day of doom. The day of reckoning for me was Friday 14th, and this day in April of 1994, will always be etched on my mind in extreme detail. Spring was in the air, the daffodils were spread like margarine across the banks, borders, and grass verges of the roads, streets, and parks of Liverpool, calling up to the dry branches, like a symphony beckoning the trees to re-spawn back to life. The nights were getting brighter, the darkness of the early morning cold winter snaps was no more. Summer was on its way, so close you could hear the grass grow, but although we now had a yard, the only grass I had to concern myself with was the herb I still smoked. Perhaps I didn't need to smoke it anymore, as there was a degree of optimism I hadn't felt without drugs for some time. Would this be a season of new beginnings? We had a new home and homelessness was not ours to worry about anymore. It wasn't a leafy affluent suburb. So what? There was something very comforting in knowing we no longer needed to second guess that knock on our door, or receive another red-letter through it. A massive weight had been lifted.

It would have been an almost perfect day, spoilt only by the fact it was Friday night, which meant work, drug dealing, and an all-nighter. This was the first time I travelled to the club from my new home. On my way there, I wondered how long it would be before I could leave this criminal disposition for good. No time like the present, I thought. We had moved, I had no excuse to sell drugs anymore. I was obviously intending to do it at least one more time, but could I make this night my last? I wasn't sure, it's hard to say no to easy cash, even if every fibre of your being is convicting you to stop what you're doing.

I was sure I was set on getting back to the life I had before dealing. Whilst college had become a complete wash-out, I had intentions of returning in September and knuckling down. If I could sit my A-levels, I was sure I could cheat again and pass them like I did my GCSEs. I missed this old normality, college, friends, recreational drugs, not having to think too hard about crime and its consequences, or needing to escape thoughts of the same. My normal now was living dead centre in this underworld I had created. Once impressive, now oppressive, it was becoming impressionably normal and I couldn't control it. Do people really enjoy breaking the law? Without drugs to keep me comfortably numb, the mess on the inside would have been seen on the outside. The thrill and spill of drugs ensured my mind didn't run away with thoughts of jail and violence, blinkered by the trappings of the criminal lifestyle that I had become accustomed to, although not as acutely as when this path to destruction began. What was painfully obvious: this scene once fulfilled my every desire. Now, I was no longer full or filled. Before drugs I was lost, in drugs found, now drugs my only comfort, but I was lost again, worse than before! I was certainly waking up to the reality that I didn't want to deal anymore, and not only because of the shock value of seeing those clubbers messed up on drugs I sold them. The only attraction left was the money. In my case, it certainly was the route to evil, a hellish existence in a bricked-up coffin. A dungeon of realisation, desolation, and isolation. 'Inevitable' is not a word in a drug dealer's vocabulary; if it were, there would be far fewer drug dealers behind bars. I once craved this life, I now craved my old life and I was now in a serious relationship with Vicki, which I wanted to grow. She gave me purpose and the comfort I could escape to.

On this very extreme night stood to attention on my drug dealing hotspot in this ridiculous bandanna, whilst I looked like a bullfighter, but the bulls making their way over to me were not on all four paws, and they were about to take me down. I was seconds away from a fight I could not win, bulls I could not escape. The police!!

Chapter 34

You're going down for 10 years!

Startled, I had been gripped and lifted off my feet. It was a smackdown, one I could not tap out of. In the bright light of the lit-up club, amongst the noise of the chattering clubbers, wondering what the hell was going on, only the sound of the turntable needle hum could be heard from the music-less speakers. The diamond-tipped needle hovered above the turntable, hanging over the record. Like the clubbers, it was itching to be dropped back onto and into the twelve inches of wax it had just abruptly left, because of me. The Ecstasy-fuelled bodies I had served earlier, waiting for the lights to drop and music to sound out once again, eager to get back to their alternative state of consciousness they had been ejected from, because of me.

Those with a front seat to this episode from The Bill fixed their gaze on to me, forgetting their need to dance momentarily, as they were offered a window into a world they had only seen on television. I may as well have been a falling star crashing through their minds, immediately entertaining, imminently too real to comprehend, I suspect the chemicals made this moment more surreal than it was. A moment I could not stop, in freefall to a place and a future that would irreversibly change me forever. For those five minutes, I became box office to these clubbers, but it gave rise to my nightmare that lasted 876,000 minutes. The time I lost and would never get back. I was their medicine man, Ebenezer Goode, now quite simply an annoyance to these clubbers. This moment was universally unimportant to them but catastrophic to me as I started out on this uncompromising, unforgiving journey into the centre of the darkest hole I had ever known before or since. I was on autopilot in survival mode, dragged out of this nightclub like a burning car from a petrol station, and at the time I wasn't sure if this was the police or gangsters. My designated pallbearers were not dressed in uniform; either way, they were carrying my coffin-less body out of this nightclub, which I once thought of as church. I am not sure I breathed too big a sigh of relief when I landed in my very own Police Mariah van. At least I knew I wasn't about to be cut open, or worse; although I certainly took some damage from these undercover policemen as they tried to disarm me.

My destination was The Main Bridewell, a Victorian dungeon, which has since been condemned. I knew we had arrived because we were no longer moving, but the engine of the Mariah van was still roaring. I could feel it vibrating through the steel floor my ear was held against. I was still face-down. Not only had I felt every bump of the road as we travelled, but also I took a few digs from the police officers, and their knees had not yet left my back. The engine came to a halt, shuddered and left without a whimper. Finally, I was picked up off the floor. I could now see my new destination. We had gone through one secure roller shutter entrance into an area with another, with an unwelcoming single iron-cased doorway ahead, the one I was about to fall through. Whilst I was standing up, I could not yet leave the vehicle until the roller shutter behind had closed. No sooner had the view from inside to out been distinguished, than my journey into this brick-walled barbed-wired beast began. But for the adrenaline pumping through my body, I would have been in pain suffered from my arrest. I left the van, one policeman in front of me and one behind, prodding and dragging me in the direction of the doorway.

Once inside, we were met by our very own welcoming committee, the drug squad, and on-duty police officers, some had been involved in the raid. Now that we were in the confines of this dungeon, the holding area, the police officers and drug squad breathed a huge sigh of relief. You could feel the tension lift. It was replaced with celebration, which strangely enough helped me to relax. Was I at a party? The shock had already taken over; what I was experiencing felt like it was happening to somebody else. All five of us had been dragged out of the club, the total sum of the drug squad's many months of graft had culminated in the capture of us. We were the trophies they had won after months of surveillance, now on display, like a victorious football team in the dressing room after the final whistle. High fives were being had all over the shop, some doing air grabs, others punching the air. Did they think I was someone else? It felt a little forced and over the top. I'm a messed-up kid escaping my past, at best an accidental gangster, not Pablo Escobar, I thought. Some of the officers would goad me, one came up close and vehemently spat out his hate for me, "We've got you, ya going down for 10 years." Why did it feel so personal? I had never met any of these policemen before. It felt like everything I had ever done wrong in my life I did personally to them. Or were they just representing all the parents of the people we sold to, in particular those two clubbers I poisoned with my drugs? Possibly…

I believe they thought they had got all of us, including Mr Big, but unsure which one of us was him. Mr Big was, of course, back at the club, probably panicking in case he was next; I was taken into a small glazed room with two policemen on either side of me. As I stood there, I could see the rest of the crew being dragged in one by one and put in similar rooms; the police clearly didn't want us together. Each one of us had to do the walk of shame to the reception desk in the centre of 4 police officers, plus one behind the reception desk asking the questions. When I was dragged out, the desk sergeant asked me if I knew why I had been arrested. I played dumb and said I didn't. Then I was asked if I had anything on me that was illegal. I confirmed no, but of course I was still carrying tablets. Only then did it dawn on me exactly where they were, in their usual place in my sister's bikini nestling behind my scrotum. I was about to be strip-searched in front of everyone. You can of course imagine my embarrassment when my trousers were pulled down, my underpants dropped, stood in this room leaning against the desk like Eddie the Eagle leaving the ski slope he had just jumped off. My arms outstretched and my hands against the edge of the desk holding me up. Centre stage quite literally unplugged, with my very own intimate 360° audience, exposed in my sister's tropical bikini bottoms, a banana sling. This particular scene was the most embarrassing situation in my life.

The policeman eventually separated me from my sister's bikini. Then counted how many tablets I had. The desk sergeant confirmed there were fifty-six and they were presumed to be tablets of Ecstasy. The desk sergeant then asked me, "Are these yours?" Surely, he knew that I would know if someone tried to sneak fifty-six Ecstasy tablets behind my sack in a banana sling. I started laughing because I didn't know what to say, which was simply nerves. The desk sergeant scowled, "What are you laughing at son, this is a serious matter, you're looking at…" Yeah, I know 10 years; it was starting to get repetitive. I nearly finished his sentence, which would have been regrettable. I'm sure they were all on a message to scare us with this 10-year threat. I now know they were laying the foundations for their coming questioning tactics. They wanted Mr Big and if 10 years was going to be the sentence, was there a deal for less if we gave him up? At this point, I was now saying no comment, as I remember The Fox shouting out to us all as we were being dragged in, "No comment, no comment". The Bumper and Hiawatha soon followed, they only had money on them, which we later found out included a load of marked notes, so they were bang to rights, and The Shotgun was the last. He had a knife, tablets, and cocaine on him. What I thought was quite odd, we all got our clothes back, and Hiawatha didn't. Somehow, he ended up in a white paper bodysuit. It looked like an adult sized "Babygro". He didn't realise he would not get a fresh pair of clothes for another four days.

Once we had effectively been signed in, we were all escorted to our rooms. I was about to spend my first night in a prison cell.

Chapter 35

The main bridewell

I had seen films and TV programmes about prison. I have also been inside a jail visiting my Dad, but nothing prepared me for the real thing, more particularly the Main Bridewell. This place played to the narrative exaggerated for effect in most prison films. I would later learn that long-term prison was not as primitive as we thought. This place was quite literally a dungeon. Talk about being thrown in at the deep end! This place was first opened in 1867, built in the Victorian tradition of striking fear into anyone who had the misfortune of spending time here, to stop them from committing crime again. It had approximately 40 usable cells each with a heavy wooden door. The cell measured 7ft x 7ft. The toilet was positioned at the end of the wooden bench I was about to sleep on, and the floors were made of stone. I later learned this jail could only be used for detention before the court as the Magistrates' buildings were adjacent, accessed by an underground passage, which I would soon travel along. This prison was completely secure. Once you were in, that was it. When I had been fingerprinted and photographed the alarm bells started to ring out: I was told to remove my belt and laces for safekeeping. Apparently, this was to prevent me from causing harm to myself.

Having left the reception desk, I was manoeuvred through another large doorway, it looked like the mouth of a yawning gorilla; the only thing missing was a drawbridge. This was a substantial jail door, built for one thing only, keeping whatever was on the other side in. This was the place I was about to spill into, (with great difficulty, as every time I made a step my foot left my shoe), and every other step my beltless jeans would slip down exposing my behind. Thankfully, the tropical print banana sling had been removed. It was kept as evidence. Had I seen the last of my sister's bikini bottoms? I did wonder whether it was likely to make an appearance as evidence in court. Thoughts of this came to life in my mind, picturing the barrister for the prosecution drawing the court's attention to Exhibit No.1, 'The Banana Sling', hanging off the end of his quill. I was ready to plead guilty to my captives to avoid such an outcome. Could you imagine, "For the benefit of the court and the jury does this belong to you Mr Cockburn?"… "Err no, it's my sister's." The barrister sighs, "Ok, were you wearing it on the said night in question."…. "Wearing what?"…. "Your sister's underwear!"… "It's a bikini, boss!"…"Okay, your sister's bikini, then!"

If only I was so brazen walking through this door. Reluctantly, I continued my path into this dungeon, nearly 150 years of history bearing down on me. I was listening for the echoes of those that once lived here, some died here, silenced by time, but not by their ghosts. Their horrific secrets were surely kept by this place. What happens in this dungeon stays in this dungeon. Was I making my own never-to-be-spoken-of story, as I walked the line, the same trodden over the last century by every sort of criminal? I was treading in the same footprints of those that had gone before me into the belly of this beast. Man alive, it was old, almost medieval. This jail specialised in the drunk and disorderly, the abusers of the abused. When I wasn't juggling my spare hand between putting my shoes back on and pulling my trousers up, I had to negotiate a rubber mattress and pillow in the other hand, plus a crusty rug I had just procured from the stores, which was going to be my bed for the next three nights.

The duty police officer pulled out his big thick key. It was like one Blackbeard would have used to open his treasure chest, rusty and spent, the keyhole big enough to climb through (if only). There was no escaping this place. The door slammed, it made me jump. The draft from its swinging heaviness pushed me further into my stone-built coffin.

The smell alone was a sentence in itself. Right there, that was deterrent enough, I would never commit another crime again. It was the stench of stale urine, the same that would knock you sick in old public toilets you would find in parks that nobody tended. As promised, at the end of the wooden bench was a steel khazi with a wooden privacy panel, for what good it did. At least it was convenient; never mind the en-suite, this was in-suite. I barely had to leave my bed to poo. Trust my luck to get the one that didn't flush properly. That was the reason why it stank. How was I going to sleep in a place like this? On the first night, I was pulled out of my tentative slumber by the arrival of my new next-door neighbour.

Each cell had a service hatch, which your food would be delivered through. Above it was an alert button in case of an emergency. The numpty in the cell next to me would not stop pressing his. In the end, the duty police officer stopped attending, which meant he was now screaming at the top of his voice, "Me meds…me @@@@ meds…. Booossssss, me meds." He wanted his medication, probably methadone; at the time I didn't have a clue what he meant. It was the thickest Scouse accent I had ever heard. It sounded like a sheet of steel being dragged across coarse gravel. He was clearly still high, but inconsolable. You could tell the police officers' patience was wearing thin. He was warned if he did not shut up and take his finger off the buzzer, next time he was getting filled in. Which was exactly what happened. This time there was more than one police officer. You could hear the smacks of knuckles against flesh as each punch made contact with this urchin's flesh, followed by screams that echoed throughout the whole of the prison, alerting everyone that someone was taking a severe beating. Now every landing in this jail was lit up like feeding time at Chester Zoo chimpanzee sanctuary.

My mind was so preoccupied with my new surroundings. Now alone, I was going to say "in the dark", but fat chance of that happening. The lights were left on 24/7, every cell was on suicide watch. In the small moments outside of the distraction of this busy place, my mind would start to wander: is this going to be my life for the next 10 years? Suddenly, I remembered my Mum was waiting at home for me. What must she be thinking, did she know yet? I said I wouldn't be late. I guess by this time it was the early hours of Saturday morning, when pubs and clubs were throwing out, so the cells were filling up. Everything echoed in this place, so every noise was amplified. How they silenced my neighbour was harrowing. You needed to be dead on your feet and deaf if sleep was going to come your way. I wasn't going to kill myself, but I was too alone and scared to be in the dark, so thankful for the bright light. When I wasn't being kept awake by the inmates, I would be catapulted out of sleep by the peephole opening and closing as the eye of a voyeuristic police officer would momentarily watch me from behind that door. The peering police officer was checking I hadn't purposely swallowed my tongue and I was still alive. It would have been the only meal worth eating. The food on offer was cold and rancid.

In those solitary moments, I could think of nothing else other than how utterly brutal this experience was so far. As a banged-up sprog, I naturally assumed this was the blueprint for the rest of my time behind bars, which of course was not helped by, "You're going down for 10 years" that kept ringing in my ears. The three-night stay dragged like anything; my only distraction was the devilment echoing around and across the place. I was unavoidably soaking up each new moment. The sound of footsteps…who were they locking up now? Are they coming for me? Somebody new had just been put in the cell next to me on the other side. It was a prostitute; she was offering the duty sergeant a deal for benefits in which he could have the 'full package' for free. I didn't sleep much the Saturday night either. I wondered where The Fox, Hiawatha, The Shotgun, and the Bumper were. I was not ready to start shouting across the landing in search of them in case I became the next victim of those police officers that dished out that brutal attack on my other neighbour, who now spoke with a whimper. I could hear his moans, the drugs were clearly wearing off, heightening the pain of that beating; he was done. I tried not to think about what I could not *stop* thinking about. It was too difficult, my overactive imagination had been switched to default mode - dread - absolutely no thought of positivity, only fear. It was horrifying. When I wasn't thinking inside my mind, every sound outside was accentuated. A screech felt like it was somebody's last breath; every bang or thud felt like it was my door about to be burst open. I had been in this room for over 30 hours, the worst grounding I had ever had.

Sunday morning came and I was greeted by two police officers saying, "Cockburn, on ya feet, NOW!" Fear gripped me. I was cuffed and dragged out of my cell. Where were they taking me?

Chapter 36

The last night of my life

Hands cuffed and being shoved down the jail-house corridors, I was taken home, not to the address I gave them when I was doing my Eddie The Eagle impression, the house we were evicted from, but to my real address.

These police officers were not about to be sent on another wild goose chase, and they didn't mind letting me know. I was bundled into an unmarked car with two coppers on either side of me. "Right, DICKHEAD, yav got one chance, where do you live?" They knew my old address, but not the new one. I thought I'd better tell them or end up a broken man, like the one in the cell next to me. They kept probing me on the way, saying "So, what ya hiding, we are going to find it." I could see the excitement in their eyes, was I Mr Big after all? They were expecting to find the engine room to our supply chain and the elusive shotgun that they probably would have known about. Thankfully, no one was home. They searched the place and finding all my steroids, confiscated them. They took several items of clothing and some cash. The clothes would evidence I sold drugs, which confused me at the time for they had me bang to rights. I later learned they were going after a conspiracy charge, which would deliver a stronger sentence than the actual supply and possession of 56 tablets they had found when I was initially brought in. I learned later that Mum was with The Bumpers mum whom she had contacted whilst looking for me, when I had not returned home as promised. This unfortunate event did momentarily bring my parents back together again as they tried to understand what happened to their son and what to do next.

As for me, I was now heading back to The Main Bridewell to be interviewed. I was first prepared by the Duty Solicitor, who explained, "Until we know the charges, you are to respond to any questions with 'no comment'." I would love to share a detailed Columbo-style take-down, but I literally have no comment. The questions that were asked were not too evasive. "Where did you get the tablets from? How long had I been selling? Did I know such and such?" They soon realised I was not Mr Big, in fact, none of us were. We were all living at home with our parents. Despite my 'no comment' delaying tactic, we were not about to discuss details, at least until we had secured proper legal representation.

We were set to appear in front of the Magistrates' courts on Monday morning. The Duty Solicitor expected the case to be adjourned, as all matters would be transferred to the Crown Court. We were definitely staying in jail if sentenced by the Magistrate, which may have been a good thing. The Magistrate could not hand down jail terms exceeding two years. Later that same Sunday, we were all charged one by one with Conspiracy to sell a Class A drug. On the advice of the Duty Solicitor, I pleaded not guilty. Ahead of Monday's meeting with the Magistrate, the Duty Solicitor confirmed he would push for bail awaiting trial but suspected such an outcome unlikely. He thought we would remain in jail on remand. Remand meant we would stay in prison until trial and sentencing. Any time served would be knocked off our sentence as time spent. Bail meant we could go free until we went to trial and were sentenced, which at that moment was preferred. I didn't want to spend another night in this dungeon, even if the outcome was inevitable.

On Monday morning, we were all held in a retaining room, together again for the first time since our arrest, which was comforting. We were then transported through the underground tunnel between the dungeon and the adjoining Magistrates' Court. Our names were called and all five of us climbed up a small staircase and sat in the dock. No sooner had I sat down, than I realised we were not alone. The general public was in attendance, plus the press; we were going to make the headlines. I saw Dad. Sitting next to him was Vicki, which melted my heart. She was holding my favourite leather jacket, which I thought was optimistic. Seeing all our families in court made it very real. Each of our Duty Solicitors put their case forward for bail, on the basis we were first-time offenders and offered no threat or danger to the general public. If the Magistrate agreed, we would accept a curfew, which meant we could not leave our homes before 8 am or after 8 pm, thus alleviating any concern of attending nightclubs and selling drugs again. The Magistrates glanced across at the prosecuting Solicitor, awaiting them to oppose. We were expecting to be remanded, but to our utter shock and amazement the prosecuting Solicitor nodded his head in agreement. The Magistrates therefore agreed to bail, but with a £1,000 surety.

Back in the holding cell, we colluded, scratched our heads, then it became clear. The reason we were offered bail was to get us back out onto the street. They knew they hadn't got Mr Big and hoped we would lead them to him. It then dawned on me: the police had confiscated what money I had left and my parents did not have £1,000. I watched each of my co-accused leave one by one. At this point, I now believed I was the only one who was staying. To my utter shock, bail had been posted by Vicki's mum. Wow, that's some introduction to your future mother-in-law. The most difficult part of the day was facing my Mum; I knew her heart would be broken yet again, this time because of me. I am going to be completely upfront: no sooner had I apologised, than I fell into Mum's arms and cried like I was 10 again. Those three nights in the Main Bridewell were more than I could handle; these were tears of relief as well as utter sadness.

The next seven months were pretty much spent getting to know Vicki, making the most of our last days together. I was too scared to break the curfew rules because I still harboured the hope of somehow getting a suspended sentence.

I would see Dave and Lee occasionally and sneak off somewhere secluded and smoke a load of weed, but time was now precious and spent mostly with Vicki. I was smitten and I had fallen in love with this beautiful girl. She had gone to her mum to save me from the torcher on remand, WOW. She had put her life on hold just to spend it with me before I went to jail, WOW. She knew I was looking at serious time, but promised to be loyal, which she was. WOW.

The Magistrates eventually referred our case to the Crown Court. Leading up to trial, we were offered a guilty plea deal, thus saving the courts and police the bother of a time-consuming trial. More seriously, we would get a third off our sentence. I suspect this was partly due to the fact the police soon realised we were not hardened criminals, even if we thought we were, and we were too scared to give up Mr Big. The day of the trial was fast approaching, but not before I had one last hoorah. If I was going down for a long time, I wanted one last night out on the town. It was Saturday night and I was to be sentenced on Monday, 31st of October - Halloween of all nights. I headed out to Birkenhead, to The Drome nightclub. It was the last weekend before my date with destiny behind bars and I was going to go out in style, with the girl I loved, on the thing I desired the most: E. Was it a fitting end to this saga? It certainly felt like it. It also felt like the last night of my life…

The next morning came and I realised I was one night away from returning to jail. I awoke on the Monday and all I'll say is, trust me - it was not a Happy Halloween.

Chapter 37

October 31st - Halloween

I didn't sleep much on the night before Halloween. How could I? The following night, mine would be a prison bed again. Screaming memories of the Main Bridewell consumed my every thought. Hyperventilating, I couldn't hide; where on earth could I run to? Was I unsavable? My three nights in the Main Bridewell were three nights too many, and I wasn't sure if my next staycation would be for five or ten years. These 28 years on, it still sends shivers down my spine. Did that really happen to me? I still wake up up in a cold sweat, catapulted out of this recurring nightmare breathing, "Huuurrrrrrr, it's ok, I'm safe, it's all over; I'm at home."

Our last slender hope of reprieve, five of us versus three Judges. The one to avoid was the one we got… What a start to the day. It was surely going to get worse. Our case was listed to be heard in the morning, so we put on a brave face and whilst we all looked like the cast of Reservoir Dogs, for what good it did us, no Judge in the land would set us free just because we wore a shirt and tie. We congregated outside the courtroom awaiting our thirty-minute warning to enter. The morning session had ended; we had to wait another hour and thirty minutes for the court to reconvene. We went to the pub restaurant, aptly named Trials, opposite the courts. We were sitting around with our families eating lunch like it could have been any other day, but painfully aware it was not any other day. This was our last day! This was our last supper! The only way we could have imagined walking out of court like this was off the back of a suspended sentence. Unfortunately, the only thing that was being suspended was our appetite, at least until our next meal, which would be in prison. We ate well, for we knew it would be some time before we would get a decent meal again.

Time flies when you're having fun or when you're trying to put off the inevitable... It was time to return to the waiting area outside the courtroom. In an attempt to steal one last intimate moment, Vicki and I stepped away from the hustle and bustle privately in the stairwell of the fire escape. We just held each other, holding back the tears, trying to stay strong for each other. It wasn't working. Pulling her in a little tighter than usual, I didn't want to let her go, closing our eyes and wishing we could wake up and everything would be ok. Fighting for every last second to remain in this embrace, I knew that any moment I would walk through the courtroom doors out of sight, never to return. The sting was unbearable. We would not hold each other again like this for a long time.

Seconds later, our solicitors confirmed the case holding up ours was wrapping up. We were given the nod to ready ourselves. Instantly, the atmosphere changed, we started saying our final goodbyes. It felt like we were being sent off to war, unsure if all of us would return. Now we were gathered in huddles with our respective families, to say one last very personal "bad bye". There was nothing good about this bye. My Mum had asked Rev. Shapland to support her, because I had no interest in God. He asked if he could pray for me: "Erm, I suppose so." For what good it would do, where were you, God, when I needed you? If you cared, why had you allowed this to happen? It was odd... The reverend started speaking about me, but not to me; for me, with his eyes closed. I looked up to see if anyone was watching. This felt uncomfortable.

No sooner had the case before ours ended, than we were rocketed into the dock. Standing room only, Dad squeezed his way in to represent me. I knew none of the people sat in the cheap seats, they were strangers waiting to be entertained at our expense. As one foot landed in the dock, I peeled my other foot off the courtroom floor, my last imprint of freedom spent! We all lined up in the dock, surrounded by a secure perspex screen. The door we walked through suddenly closed and was locked; we were now detained! A door we would never use again, one of many here-on in, locked behind me. We would be leaving by the doorway to the left, down a small staircase. It was being readied by the shadow of the prison officer. No sooner had I stood to my feet; than the Judge entered. A slight but mature man, who carried himself with great authority. He was extremely well-spoken, but a man of few words. It wasn't his time yet; but it was eerie to finally meet our executioner, intentionally unrecognisable, hidden under his red gown, and white silky wig. He had a pair of half-moon spectacles, which he kept peering over to glare at us from the underside of his ruffled eyebrows.

This wasn't a trial; we had already pleaded guilty. we were simply going through the motions to get us to a place where a sentence could be meted out and judgement cast down. When all representations had been made, the Judge stepped away to consider the sentencing he had already considered. The reality, he was having a cup of PG Tips in the comfort of his chambers. Now he was back and we all moved to the edge of our seats, gulped, holding our breath like a team of well-drilled synchronised swimmers. "PLEASE STAND FOR SENTENCING!"

The moment we had all been waiting for had arrived. Silence came crashing down like a feathered sledgehammer. We were ready, no we weren't, yes we were, let's just get it done, braced in any event, now trying to listen with our eyes and see with our ears, as The Judge was NOT about to get to the point. I was expecting a number followed by years, done and dusted. Did we really need a road map to his decision that he didn't want to reveal just yet? The Judge had taken his leadoff Chris Tarrant about to confirm the answer to the million-pound question the contestant had just got right. Did it really have to be this tense?

The only thing missing was a drum roll. This Judge loved the sound of his voice, dipping in and out of case law like a seasoned pugilist, referring to many similar cases like an airport lost-luggage attendant, and all with the deep seriousness he must rely upon in determining our fate, if only he would just tell us the outcome. It was taking too long: he should just put us out of our misery.

Like a nuclear reactor that was about to overheat, I shut down! I stopped listening, although I could hear every utterance from the mouth of this silver-tongued wordsmith. In my confusion, all I heard was 14, plus a deafening silence that let out long............ YEARS! The air instantly exploded from my lungs like a burst balloon. I couldn't breathe, shock kicked in. My knees started to tremble; was I about to faint? I gripped the edge of the dock parapet to steady myself, but I wasn't ready to hit the deck just yet. How can it be 14 years, we were told a maximum of 10 years, and a third off, not added to it? This theatre of dread playing out in my head, so loud, drowned out the sound of this executioner's voice; his every syllable now deafened by the death rattle in my mind. In a rare moment of clarity, I learned that The Shotgun had got 10 years. But he was done on three counts, possession of cocaine, a knife, and the only thing I was charged with, conspiracy to sell Ecstasy, so why was his sentence less than mine? I finally got my breath back, and turned to see my Dad, who looked like I felt. His face confirmed my worst nightmare. I looked for comfort in numbers and secured the attention of The Bumper, I uttered the words through gritted teeth in disbelief, "FOUR..... TEEN... YEARS!" He looked at me in astonishment, taken aback. Like me, he couldn't quite reconcile what I had just said. He then dragged me kicking and screaming back to reality .... "MONTHS, YA BELTER, not years." "WHAT! Say again," I replied utterly confounded. "The Judge said MONTHS, not years." I got it so wrong! Instant elation, ready to drop to my knees like I had scored the winning cup final goal with the last kick of the game. I had gone from harbouring hopes of a suspended sentence, to 14 years. Hiawatha glanced at me with disdain. He couldn't understand why I was buzzing. "What's wrong with you?" "14 months, back of the net, YEAH!" I excitedly declared a mid-air grab. He said, "NOoooo," now shaking his head like a wet dog, "40....FOUR ZERO MONTHS, ya melt!" Whilst, it certainly wasn't 14 years, I was plunged back into despair, sending me falling into my chair. This was the biggest number I had heard yet, this was 26 more than 14. At this point, I didn't know whether I was coming or going.

We actually got three years and four months. In my head, I was trying to work out how many Christmases I would be away for; of all the things I made a priority. What about, would Vicki wait that long? When I finally arrived at the certain realisation it wasn't 14 years, or 40 months, we would only do half the term if let out early on good behaviour, 20 months still felt like a long time. Let's be clear here, 20 months on the outside is not the same. Believe me when I say that inside, one day feels like a week on the outside.

All five of us were marched down below and placed in individual holding cells. We were allowed to say a final farewell to our family from behind a protective screen. As I was 21, the oldest of the gang I was going to an adult jail. I was called sooner than everyone else to board my hearse, the prison bus. I came up out of the bowels of the Crown Court and exited right, past the Albert Dock. I got to see the beauty of a disappearing sunset for what would be the last time in a long while. It felt like the final curtain over my life, draping and shadowing the most scenic part of Liverpool as I passed the three Graces on the waterfront, the Liver Birds waving me off. I was about to flap my wings but in no time at all, I arrived at my cage: HMP Walton.

Chapter 38

HMP Walton, England

HMP Walton is a fortress, a larger version of the Main Bridewell. The prison consists of 1002 cells, and 30 dark cells known as solitary confinement. The population fluctuates around 1400 inmates across 8 wings. The prison was once the site of 62 judicial executions. The last was that of Peter Anthony, convicted for murder, and hanged on 13 August 1964. I later learned he was on '*I Wing landing 2*', you've guessed it, the exact place I was to spend most of my time in this jail…

All twelve of us were all called one by one to be formally sworn in, like generals of our 7 by 7 stone-built coffins, the ones we were soon to be unloaded into. The officer on the desk confirmed I was now known as 'FN3698': the first stage of processing complete. I was then led into an area and asked to undress in front of two male prison officers in order that they could check if I had anything hidden inside my backside. This highly embarrassing situation was now the second time I had been fully naked in front of strangers. Unfortunately, it would not be the last. (Because my crime was drugs-related, every time I had a family visit, which was fortnightly, before heading back to my cell, I was required to drop my kit to be inspected again, and again, and again…)

We were all going to different wings. My destination, *I Wing Level 2*, you now know was the execution deck. Too long, alone in the darkness of my cell, was spent thinking on that… 62 people hanged in the immediate vicinity where each night I tried to get to sleep. This wasn't helped when one inmate claimed an entity could be seen, on my landing, of a hanging man kicking his legs about as the noose broke his neck slowly strangling its victim. I was placed smack bang in the middle of this building's grim history. Such a place of corporal and capital punishment is bound to have its fair share of ghost stories. Enter the Victorian prison warder: Apparently, he would come through the locked door of prisoners' cells in the dead of night and pull men from their bunks. The click of the warder's foot studs could be heard on the walkway outside the cell doors of its victims. Those with eyes to see would find a man standing over them dressed as a prison warder with a huge black handlebar moustache. If the inmate tried to escape, his throat would be gripped hard by the ghost's icy cold hand, until he could take no more…then the figure would vanish. On other occasions, this handlebar-moustached entity would turn up brandishing what looked like a huge riot baton, which he used to strike the walls and the beds of the cell he was haunting. One story detailed how an inmate was cornered and screamed out, "In the name of Jesus Christ, get out of here!" The figure turned around immediately, swiftly marching through the solid locked door. His studs could be heard walking into the distance, click-click, as this antiquated prison warder from a bygone era vanished…

Once I'd had all my cavities checked, I was given my uniform: a striped shirt, blue jeans, and a blue jumper, with brown plastic dancing shoes that had absolutely no grip. I of course got socks and underwear; whilst they were crispy clean, the thought that others had used them still made me shudder. I then took my outside clothes back to the desk and signed them into a box known as my personal belongings. They would only be returned to me on the day I left this prison. I was then led away to see the doctor, who wanted to discuss whether I had any STDs or addictions and illnesses that needed tending to, amongst other invasive questions. Finally, I was photographed and fingerprinted again.

I went to the store, collected my bedding, some toiletries and eating utensils, then I was escorted through my first gated grill iron doorway

towards *I Wing Level 2*. It was starting to feel like a dungeon... Being
the farthest section of the jail, I got the tour of the place. It was a lot
cleaner than the Main Bridewell: you could smell the disinfectant.
It must have been close to 9 pm as I ventured through... There was
certainly a lot of noise, but not to the extreme as there was at the Main
Bridewell. That was partly because most inmates there hadn't just rolled
in off the street drunk and disorderly; they were living here. Like the
Main Bridewell, the reason why this place was never condemned was
due to an overhaul undertaken in 1974, which brought it up to the
minimum standard. This only satisfied the authorities; it did not improve
the quality of an inmate's life, which was horrendous, as I was about
to experience. (Each year on average, over 300 inmates self-harm in
this place and 6 inmates are found dead. Many take their own lives.
More recently, three inmates died within three weeks of each other, one
within 48 hours of arriving.) In 2017, this jail was declared the worst
in the UK. When I was there it was bad; even 'slop-out' still existed,
which meant you used a bucket in your room to go to the toilet.

I finally got to my room, which was not too dissimilar to the cell in
the Main Bridewell, other than the window was bigger. It still had
bars, and the toilet thankfully, was not a bucket or in-suite, it was en-
suite. I surveyed my surroundings. I had a sideboard, a chair, and a
small desk. The walls were painted yellow; I wasn't too sure if this was
the colour, or the stain of cigarette and tobacco smoke. In those days,
smoking inside was allowed. I learned I was going to have a cell mate,
but he was currently in a court in Wales on trial for Armed Robbery.
I wouldn't see him until the weekend. Remembering this was still
Monday night gave me some time to come to terms with the fact that
I was sharing a bunk bed and a toilet with a complete stranger; more
to the point, a convict.

I made my bed, taking the bottom bunk, which is usually the privilege
of the hardest person in your cell, which was me; I was the only one
in it! Apparently, the top bunk was less desirable. I peered out of the

window to see if I had a view, I didn't, other than a mirror image of what I was in, which was K wing, the only wing that did 'slop out'. If you caused trouble, this is where you would go. Trust me when I say, I was highly motivated to avoid the exercise of posing in a bucket in public, so I was on my best behaviour. This window became my TV on canteen day when inmates could spend their wages and personal money. I would witness many lines with goods attached as payment for drugs. It was bed linen that had been ripped into thin rope-like slivers and tied together for length. On the end of these makeshift lines, items such as tobacco, phone cards (the currency of jail), and drugs were being transferred from one cell window to another, intricately fed from one landing to another. It was almost marvellous; the ingenuity of this transport system was a sight to see, a primeval version of Amazon. If the destination was on the same landing, the sender would swing the line like a lasso until it was in reach and the recipient would hold his arm out through the bars until the line wrapped around it, and payment or shipment was made. I would always wait for the reaction when somebody would nab it before it got to the correct person.

On this Halloween night, no one was celebrating and most of the inmates had settled down for the night - so I thought I would give it a try. At least I had control of the lights this time and of course, if I needed help, there was that special button Mr Meds played his tune on that night in the Main Bridewell. I had absolutely no intention of pressing this, or alerting any screw any time soon. I didn't want to put the light out just yet; in fact, I didn't want to sleep in the dark. I undressed and climbed into my bed, a proper scratcher. It had been well and truly lived in by the many inmates who lay in this place before me, crawling with their DNA and all manner of itchy things left behind, with only a thin sheet membrane protecting me from their carbon body print. The shape moulded by the previous recipient was deep, he was much bigger than me, so it was ridiculously uncomfortable. The bed-sheet consisted of an under-cover, top cover, a crusty rug, and a hard pillow. These had been thoroughly cleaned and starched, you could smell it, and the sheets were almost crispy. I could hear the television the night guard was watching on the landing. Big Ben sounded out; it was News at Ten. I realised this is the closest I will be getting to television for the foreseeable future. Today, inmates have TVs and Playstations in their pads, but in those days none of these were allowed. I spent 10 years of my life in a cult that prohibited me from owning or watching a TV. Now, I was in this prison cell, which the cult had certainly had a hand in putting me in. Finally and reluctantly, I laid my head on the pillow, looked up at the underside of the bunk bed above, and started to weep. I had never felt so lonely, exasperated, desperate and scared by how daunting the future looked. As far as I was concerned, I had no future. I am not ashamed to say I cried myself to sleep that night. I was absolutely spent; the whole experience had taken its toll. Through my tears, I fell asleep quickly.

Chapter 41
24 Hour bang up

My first morning was like every other morning in Walton HMP, woken by the sound of violins, otherwise known as my iron cell door crashing in and open by my very own special concierge. If there was a prison officer's brass band you knew this guy was on the cymbals. He had been up long before he wanted to be, so he still had his bed on his back and the bit between his teeth, burdened by the early shift short straw. His job was to get me and all my neighbours out of our scratchers for a very special, but classical, continental breakfast. My alarm door would always go off around 7.00 am: I didn't have to worry about getting up too late; this was a bedside service. I had 30 minutes to get dressed and collect my morning smorgasbord of nourishment. The servery was in the middle of the landing and would serve the whole wing 200+ men, so there was always a queue. Usually, when you queue like this it was going to be worth the wait. Unfortunately, on this occasion, the queue was due to the situation we were all in. If we didn't eat, our stomachs would need surgically peeling off our backs. Boredom accompanied by starvation was an excruciating combination, the boredom made you hungrier, and the hunger magnified the boredom.

Every day was 'à la carte' day. Each item of handmade freshly prepared warmed-up food had its very own special place in its dedicated compartment on a state-of-the-art indestructible glistening silver tray, which was transportable: I could take it away with me. I could eat its contents in the comfort of my chamber. The array of freshly defrosted produce usually comprised a delicately dried bread slice. It didn't have to be toasted, its texture was like toast, but it had not felt the heat of an electric element or similar since the day it was baked in an oven. It seemed to be specially preserved to keep it fresh, which gave it a resolute yet crispy toast-like consistency. This wasn't any old toast, this was HMP Walton toast. It was as if it had been dry-cured and matured to palatable perfection, complemented with a fresh thumb of specially-selected lard. This soft knob was as pure and white as the driven snow; in fact, it was translucent. It went down a treat and ensured anything I eat exited me deep-fried the following morning. There was usually a specially prepared heat-resistant oeuf: it had been boiled that long it was a chicken's beak away from hatching. The yellow yolk was infused with a luminous grey patina. There was always porridge, lashings of this thick rich stuff; it was a white gold that just melted in your mouth. The leftovers were too special to throw away, and used to repair erosion and corrosion of the cement degradation within these 19th-century walls and floors throughout the halls of this University of Life. Occasionally, we would get a deep-fried spam fritter: what a treat, slow-cooked, and heated to utter perfection, submerged in its own juices that glistened from the surface. There was no need for garnish. Mine was extra rare and extra salt would magically release its tongue-dehydrating flavours: it just fell away in your mouth. Picture me snuggling my lips on the inside of my fist blowing a big fat kiss and throwing it up into the air like a French Michelin-starred chef, Mmwaaahh! This cuisine always came with the compliments of the chef, who I never got to thank for this daily festival of delectable taste sensations. The humility of this super-talented nutriment agitator was admirable. In a nutshell, it was flavourless stodge that you had to eat, or starve.

My cell had been upgraded to include a silver service collection. When I finished, I could leave the tray on the floor outside my door and it would be collected and cleaned without me lifting a finger, but not before the percussion section of the prison brass band had returned and locked me back up again. Usually around 11:00 p.m., I would receive a special invitation to amble around the grounds of this castle in a dedicated, but very secluded haven, each wing of this palatial residence had one. It was invitation only, the public were not allowed to walk around this tarmacadam secret grassless garden, offset and framed by a complimentary but sprawling high steel acoustic yellow mesh fence, which magnificently towered into the air, nobody was getting in or past this simple, but effective, display of highly skilled engineering and ironmongery. This recreational enlightenment was available without prejudice. You had the option to experience this wonderment in three different settings: rain, wind, or shine. Each experience was tailored to utter perfection purposely, to enhance the remaining 23 hours of the day. It was an opportunity I would make the most of. Forgoing the pleasure of my chamber without interruption didn't come at a price, but what a treat, what a retreat; and it didn't cost me a penny.

Once a week I was spoilt rotten. It was a ticket-less event, but limited availability only. It was part of the package deal I had secured on entry: the chance to watch classic cinematography in full living and breathing technicolour. Blockbusters such as Lassie, and the Swiss Family Robinson, enjoyed in this magnificent acoustically enhanced venue, experienced from the lower ground floor of this 4-storey cavernous atrium. The surround sound effects were sublime; this wasn't artificially enhanced, this was a real-time echo with authentic background noise, which meant you almost knew what was being said by the actors, although thankfully not at the cost of stealing this special experience. I had carte blanche to imagine what was going on and what was being said. We weren't just watching, we were participating. I was an inadvertent scriptwriter filling in the gaps where you could not hear. It was a very unique and exclusive way to enjoy these movies like never before. Thank God I couldn't lip read, but they were clever: the screen was purposely placed at a distance, and adapted so it was big enough to see what was going on but small enough there was not a cat's chance in hell the audience could decipher and read the characters' lips. The attention to detail was astonishing, outstanding; no stone had been left unturned. This was signature living. If only in keeping with the heightened positivity, which was far from the reality, what I experienced was indistinct negativity. This was a deeply depressing and despairing place. You don't live here…you don't even exist. You survive.

Going back to that first day: walking through the empty corridors was a stark contrast to the very first morning stepping out of my cell and seeing the landings full of many people dressed like me. It was like an ants' nest, inmates crawling everywhere. My very first cellmate, better known as my pad mate, was called Gareth. He had been in jail several times and was expecting his next sentence to be handed down for armed robbery 8-10 years. He held up a bookmaker with a shotgun. Despite seeing very little of him, I found he was a decent enough fella and he tried to encourage me as much as he could. He sympathised, he knew I was a prison sprog and struggling. I was two weeks in, and apart from the weekend, I had spent nearly every waking hour by myself. Alone with nothing but my thoughts, worrying about worrying.

Things took a turn for the worse in my third week. You remember that firm we went toe to toe with? Two of them were now held on remand on the same wing as I was. Even though I was now back down to around 11 stone and my hair was shorter so I looked different, that didn't quell my nerves, so I stopped taking association and the 1-hour walks in the yard. Within a week of these gangsters arriving it was reported somebody had taken some damage by way of the PP9 attack. This was a large heavy long-life battery, which was square, the size of a Rubik's cube and with two spring conductors on the top. The corner edges were sharp, and when this battery was placed in a pillowcase it became an impressive weapon. The victim would be left with a deep right-angled indentation, usually in their skull; attacks would unsuspectingly come from behind. This was a deep abrasion and blood would pour everywhere. Stitches were always required. Bullets were also found on our wing. Had they been brought in by those gang members? Were they for me because they had recognised me? Obviously, my broken mind ran away with itself. The officers naturally believed there may be a gun to accompany these bullets. As a consequence, we were all placed on 24-hour lockdown. I didn't shower for 2 weeks, nor did I receive a fresh change of clothing. This also meant my weekend cellmate couldn't return to keep me company. This was when things really started to worsen for me.

Although your freedom is taken away, the real prison is in your mind. What do I mean? We can often go to bed tired, lay our head down to rest, and start thinking about that one thing that is a worry. It could be a bill you can't pay, job insecurity, or even an argument you wish you never had. All of a sudden, these thoughts mushroom, and it's all you can think about. You're wide awake, riddled with fear. You eventually fall asleep, wake up the next day and get back to life comfortably numb, sufficiently distracted for it not to matter anymore, even if for a glancing moment you recall the night before wondering why you couldn't sleep. In jail, there is no life to get back to, and the worry just escalates because it's all you can think about, all of the time. One of three things happen to most people in prison (not all); one, they kill themselves; two, supernatural power lifts them out of their mental mire and changes them forever, (unfortunately, this is not a regular occurrence), or three, they bite their lip and just about get through it, but often come out more bitter and twisted than when they went in, with too many returning to this unwanton place. Do you know you can be in jail imprisoned by four walls but set free? Similarly, you can be free but imprisoned within the four walls of your mind. Mentally, the latter is far worse because prison time is limited to your sentence. Mental imprisonment can be forever.

This point in my life was the start of what took me quickly to the end of my rope, a place of total despair. In my messed-up head, I was going to die in jail, somebody was going to hurt me. What if my parents died like theirs and I couldn't attend the funerals, or spend time with them as a free man again? Was this stress-induced sickness that I felt, or even cancer? Thick overpowering dark nonsense, demonic whispers and lies of satan consumed me. I was drowning in a sea of dread and I simply didn't want to live anymore.

Chapter 40
The devil's playground

All that time alone in my cell took its toll. Every minute felt like an hour, an hour felt like a day, a day like a week, a week like a month, and it simply felt like I had years ahead of me. My only comfort was no comfort at all: mealtime, those small minutes collecting my food when i was no longer alone. I was of course getting letters from my family and Vicki, but I am not sure they helped. All they did was remind me of what I was missing. I distinctly remember listening to and watching from my cell window all the fireworks go off and explode in the night sky on November the 5th. This display felt exaggerated in the extreme as if sent to demonstrate what I was missing, how abnormal my life had become, and how normal life was outside, teasing me. It was in touching distance but untouchable, it was cruel. I also had the company of a small yellow transistor radio my Dad had sent in, but again, whilst somewhat of a distraction, it was only reminding me of the outside world I could not be part of. This started to feel like that time as a kid when I was imprisoned within the cult. Plus, the last time I was so enamoured by a little radio like this, was my first worldly experience when we escaped the cult and I celebrated Captain Sensible going to number 1. What a long way back to the top I had so unceremoniously skydived from! Like then, this little radio was creating a soundtrack to my life, but this time it was in prison, a soundtrack I didn't want to relive or remember. What a contrast!

Thankfully, these gangsters were soon moved off our wing, although two weeks of 24 hours bang-up had left its mark. I was not only imprisoned by the surrounding walls of this cage but now by my mind, which was far worse. I was imprisoned in a prison. I had lost all ability to think rationally, and every thought was unedifying, discouraging, fear-driven and would take root, spreading in my mind like cancer.

On this particular day, I came back from my walk around the yard. As I was walking towards my pad, the door was shut. That was unusual, it should have been open as I was on exercise. Not only was it shut, but someone was banging from the other side. The closest thing to an angel arrived in my cell. It may as well have been, because what I needed the most was company; more so, a familiar face who had been in this place before, someone I could trust, who could lift me out of the deathly mire I was now hanging over, held only by a thread. It was Mad Roy. The screw had stopped listening to the buzzer so Roy was now banging, which he stopped as soon as he saw me. Even though at this point I was unsure God even existed, Roy felt like a gift sent supernaturally, as if somebody upstairs was now looking out for me, finally. I didn't even know Roy was in this prison and of all 1002 cells he could have been relocated to, he was put in mine. In reality, Roy couldn't have been more diametrically opposed to that of an angel, but he was exactly what I needed at the exact time I needed it. This guy had done plenty of bird, and he was on remand for selling weed. Because he had a record as long as his arm, in and out of youth centres, borstals, and prison all his life, when he was arrested there was no chance of getting bail. The reason why he had been moved into my cell from another landing is that he was found hiding in his cupboard when he should have been elsewhere, with a lit spliff hanging out of his mouth. His punishment was a move to the execution landing with me. It was only then I realised that where I was stationed was actually a punishment, one to avoid, (particularly if you believed in ghosts). We knew each other well enough for me to be able to be completely honest with him. Mad Roy effectively grabbed me by the scruff of the neck and saved me from falling back into an open grave of dread, which I was hanging over seconds before he arrived.

For two weeks we spent every hour together playing chess, cards, chatting, sharing stories, smoking weed, yes, smoking weed - something that could have got me a thirty-day extension. However at that moment, I didn't care. The next two weeks flew, but it would be the last time, at least whilst I remained under lock and key, that time would fly. The fate-based appointment with Roy was simply an Elastoplast over an enormous gaping bleeding wound. Despite his unheavenly-like disposition I could not help but wonder, had he really been sent by God to help me? That was until the day the Chaplain did his usual visits, opened our door, and asked if we needed prayer or help at all. Mad Roy revealed his privates, pointed to something rather unsavoury at its tip and asked the prison chaplain, "Can you help me with this?" I knew then, Roy was surely not a messenger from God, but had God positioned him to provide me with some sanity in that dire time of my life?

No sooner had Roy exposed himself than he was moved. I had a new cellmate whose name was Fred. Fred was from Wales, in his late 50s, and he was a smackhead (heroin addict). He was also a rockabilly and looked like he combed his hair with a toffee apple. He had a head on him like a ship's cat. He had one eye facing the door and the other the ceiling, it wasn't because he was smacked up, he had a ridiculous turn in his eyes that was set at quarter to two. Despite him being a drugy, he was a thoroughly decent chap although on remand for serial shoplifting. I was heartbroken for the guy though. He had no family; he would tell me how most of them had died prematurely. This was the reason he hid in heroin use and abuse. He shoplifted to feed his habit. Fred stayed with me as a welcome cellmate for two weeks, before he was moved on to somewhere else. As for me, finally I was going to get to escape the execution wing: a bed had come up on the U wing. The placement also came with a job, and a decent job at that. I thought it was exactly what I needed, However it turned out to be the worst thing I could have got...

Chapter 41
The end of my rope

The new job was on the servery, which meant I was out of my cell from 7 am to 7 pm. My duties included serving food to the inmates, collecting trays, distributing razors, and cleaning the landings. It paid £12 a week, only bettered by working in the kitchen, and also the "shit parcel" brigade. Inmates two'ed up on K wing: if one pooed the other was not going to sit and bask in its ambience, so it was launched out of the window, usually wrapped up. Hence there was a special team of well-paid collectors. Whilst I was out of my cell, most of the day when I wasn't two officers who had it in for me would turn over my pad regularly, which of course I shared with another. I was specifically targeted because I was in for drugs, so quite naturally, they thought I would be bringing drugs into the prison. They would get me to do the usual humiliation drop, naked, in my pad, then they would pull out all my letters and empty their contents in case anything was hidden in the envelopes, throwing mine and my pad mates mattress off our beds. The cell was turned upside down. It started to put a rift between me and my new pad mate who was a Mancunian. He didn't need my turnover inconvenience to put him in a bad mood, it made him twice as bad, so he became very difficult to live with. He would go several days and not speak to me. When he did talk he would release one flippant comment or another. Often, he was just plain nasty. Living together on top of each other became unbearable. I'm not sure how long we could have gone on like that. I was starting to worry he might do something to me in my sleep. We didn't really speak anyway so I didn't know what he was in for. I can't even recall his name.

When another pad came up, more particularly on the servery landing, I pleaded with Shoony Shies Webster for a relocation. He was the screw that ran the servery, his second name was Webster, a proper sergeant major so his shoes were ultra-shiny. He was very regimented but funny. If he caught me leaning on the wall taking a break he would ask me, "How long did you think that wall had been there?" I knew the answer, "150 years, boss." "That long? Then why the @@@@ did it need you to keep it up," Shoony Shies would proclaim, in other words, stop leaning on it and get back to work. I was responsible for cleaning landing 3 and collecting their trays. When I finished cleaning and dusting, Shoony Shies would put a pair of white gloves on and start stroking and feeling the edges of the corridors. He looked like a Parisian mime artist. The white gloves would show me up to be a liar, at least at first. Of course, I would have to start again. I pleaded with him to move me, which he drew out in typical comical fashion, knowing he had already arranged to relocate me in any event. It was normal that those who worked on the servery lived on the same landing, usually in the immediate vicinity. Thankfully, I was relocated, which was a massive weight lifted, as I had begun to dread the end of each day returning to be with that poisonous imp. This experience again left its mark, and simply added to the increasing tension that was building up within me. Living with somebody who didn't want you there was just as lonely and as disparaging as being by myself, if not worse. Actually, it was lonelier, and deeply affecting. The release from this situation made my first Christmas day in jail a little more bearable. My new situation was undeniably improved, but waking up on Christmas day in 1994 was just awful: the first in 21 years without my family, still today my favourite day of the year. I wanted to curl up in bed and remain there until the day had passed, but because of my job, that was not possible.

The arrival of New Year's Eve welcomed in 1995, which meant I could declare, "I am going home next year," for what comfort it served; it didn't make me feel any better. Whilst New Year's Eve was not as bad as Christmas Day, locked behind my cell door in the dark, I did begin to dream about what I would have been doing this time last year, although I was reminded about those two clubbers who took my drugs and fell ill. I also remember how, when we had finished selling that night we were allowed to party in this club, and how I welcomed in 1994 off my head, euphoric. Little did I know a year later, I would be in the dark of a prison cell thinking about that night. The whole prison seemed to be in a mood of celebration; for a lot of inmates this was the year, they would be getting out. The only other times this place lit up like it did on New Year's Eve, was firstly when the football was on, everybody would listen on their radio, and if your team scored you would start banging on your door. The other time would be when a nonce, paedophile, more colloquially known as a beast, would be transported to the hospital wing from A wing through U wing, the only route to their destination. They couldn't pass until everyone was behind their door and locked in. Because of this exercise in protecting the identity of this said inmate, everybody knew what was happening and who was travelling through. The scene on this wing at those moments were horrific because everyone to a man was now stood behind their door hitting and kicking it as loud as possible, constantly hissing and screaming, "Beast, beast, beast, beast, beast, beast." It was one of the most surreal experiences I ever did witness. If this experience didn't stop them reoffending, I don't know what would.

I had been in jail for just over two months. At this moment, the outside and freedom had become a distant memory. Despite the fact I was now out of my cell with less time to dwell on the lies my imagination kept telling me, there was always something that I had to worry about. When I was in the resumed safety of my cell again alone with my thoughts, mentally I was under attack. This brain drain was taking its toll. I was one more crisis, situation, circumstance, consuming thought away from a complete breakdown; I was losing it: had I already lost it? I believed I had cancer because I was losing blood every time I went to the toilet. When you're suffering from stress, the weakest part of your body gives in the quickest.

The job paid well and meant that I was out of my cell every day, most of the day; more particularly in the evening when most notably other inmates weren't. Once we had finished up on the servery and cleaned it down, I went to my respective landings to collect the empty dinner trays from outside of each cell. I started to dread canteen days. An outside line can only be thrown from one room to the other if on the same side of the landing. What happens if that destination was on the other side of the landing? The fact that I was not banged-up meant on canteen day I was the only way a dealer could get gear from one room across the landing to another. The first time went a bit like this. "Psst, lad, psst lad, PSST LAD," obviously the voice had got my attention. I knew what was coming; I then had to work out which door it was coming from. "Over here, DICKHEAD!" You don't know who's behind the door, so you don't run the risk of ignoring the caller. "Do you know who I am?" I didn't get the chance to answer. I feared if I didn't do what I was told he was going to open me up. "Take this to number 47 and bring me back the right amount of phone cards." If I was caught with what I now had in my possession… Assuming it was drugs, three phone cards for this very small parcel, after doing my math, meant it could only be heroin. I was on a knife's edge. I remember what happened to Fred that time he was sold brick dust. What if this was brick dust? How would I know? Surely it would be me that would be getting shivved or PP9'ed in the morning. If it was legit, I couldn't risk taking back only two phonecards, or even worse, used phonecards, because then I would be indebted to this dealer, who would do the same. Furthermore, what if a screw caught me. Can you imagine! This wasn't a straw breaking the camel's back; this was a caravan of camels breaking my back.

If I got caught, I would have to do all 40 months of my sentence, and next time it would not be a minimum term or a third off, it would be 5+ years. If I said no, delivered brick dust, or brought back the wrong amount of phone cards, I was sure I would be Mars-barred. The very special carving instrument of choice was a toothbrush, which had been melted and two Bic razor blades inserted in its head, side by side about 2mm apart and it would leave the victim with the same pattern usually reserved for the top of the chocolate bar. I didn't want to get striped by this instrument, so I did what I was told. The slasher would usually sneak up from behind, or just casually walk alongside their victim at meal time, or in the exercise yard, and quickly swipe this double-bladed toothbrush across the victim's face. If not done correctly it could nick the victim's neck possibly the main artery, the jugular; at least that's how it played out in my mind. Regardless, there would be blood pouring everywhere, scarring the victim forever physically and mentally. I felt trapped yet again, but this time shackled dead centre in the middle of the devil's playground. I was a drug dealer sent to jail, effectively dealing drugs in jail. Furthermore, I couldn't stop this blood emission from my behind, it was getting worse at this point I didn't know what was causing it so I thought it was cancer.. The least of my worries was not if I would die, but when? I wondered if it was the best option because I couldn't take this anymore. I was now losing the will to live; this was just brutal. I was getting it all ends up from all sides. My family had front row seats witnessing my deterioration when they visited. Every other week they saw me I looked a little worse, spoke a little less, lost a little more weight… I was dying inside. Vicki remembers one of her last visits to this place, how I struggled to lift my head, and spoke in one-word syllables. I was completely broken; I had come to the end of my rope.

Chapter 42

Frank!

My Mum had a friend who knew someone called Frank Matthews, a prison worker. Frank was in his 60s when I met him and had given up his retirement to focus on helping prisoners. This meant he could arrange to meet me on a chaplaincy visit. I didn't have to use up a visiting order. Frank was a softly-spoken gentleman with a rich Scouse accent. He was unlike anybody I had met before. He carried himself in a dignified manner with authority but was very unassuming, and the humility of this man was evident to see. The only thing I didn't take to, he was a Bible basher, Jesus freak, a member of the God squad. Mum insisted that I meet Frank because she was so worried about me, so I agreed. The mood I was in, I didn't really want to see anyone, more particularly someone representing God, the silent God, the one that stole 10 years of my life in the cult, the one that never answered a single one of my prayers as a kid, the one I took so much stick for as a school kid, the one that ran that cult, the one that took my Dad twice, the one that buried my grandparents despite us, split my family up, the one that was responsible for losing our family home, intent on ruining my life, the one that was sending me to hell, the reason I was in this place suffering immeasurably. The unavoidable truth was, Mum was part of God's plan - this God, whom later I was to meet personally and realise I had totally the wrong perspective of. Sending Frank to see me was a divine appointment. I said Yes, as a change of scenery was appreciated. Little did I know I was being drawn by the Holy Spirit, Whom I now know as my friend. My soul was groaning

and crying out on my behalf to the heavens to be saved, and to be
freed from the darkness oppressing me. Spiritually, I was desolate,
parched, deserted, in need of restitution. The strangling weeds of satan's
wilderness were suffocating my soul. In his playground, I had become
his subject; his star pupil, and I didn't know it. He wanted me on the
end of my bedspread, hanging from the ceiling, and he was not going
to let me up until he had ended me. He knew that if he could get me
to the end of my rope, I would place myself on the end of his rope,
the point of no return: a position of utter destitution. It would be an
easy way out. He was intent on making it my only way out. It was one
of two options I had left.

The second option, I was about to find out.

I once heard of a testimony about a man who did not believe in God
or Jesus, but had a dream that changed this. In that dream, there was
a white fence that ran straight down the middle of a luscious green
field. In the dream, this man was sitting on the fence wondering why
either side was so full of nature's reserve yet only he and this fence were
taking centre stage. Jesus turned up with his followers on one side,
then satan with his on the other, separated only by the fence which
the man was sat on. During this spiritual showdown, Jesus only had
eyes for the man and said, "I LOVE YOU," waited for a response, and
then departed. In his evil satan, turned his gaze to the man still sat on
the fence and said, "You're coming with me!" The man said, "I didn't
choose you." "That fence is mine," satan declared! The man woke from
his dream and gave his life to Jesus. What does that even mean? How
do you give your life to Jesus? Frank was about to tell me. I warmed to
Frank straight away. He was a friendly face in this extremely unfriendly
place. There was something different about him, and he knew how
to pick his moments to bang on about God. As you can appreciate,
God was not on my priority list, but Frank told me I was on God's,
as he was especially fond of me. In his company, I felt safe. Being in
his presence was like stepping out of the cold into a warm room. The

voices that continually haunted my mind quietened. This made it easier to listen, even though I knew he was about to bang on about Jesus. I also listened because I did not have much to say. I couldn't share what I was doing, or what I was involved in; imagine if it got back to my Mum. To speak the same to anyone was tantamount to being called a grass, and in jail, there is only one thing worse than grass, a nonce. Frank's demeanour was so engaging that I wanted to listen. He made me feel important and loved. For the last 3 months, I had become a number, unloved and of little importance. This Jesus Frank was telling me about apparently loved me, thought I was worth dying for, would take me as I am with all my baggage and rubbish. He wasn't waiting for me to get right or clean first. He had died on the cross to **make** me clean, free from sin and evil. I was already acceptable to Him. Frank told me God had been pursuing me all my life. He knew me before the foundation of the earth. He knit me in my mother's womb and loved me with a passion. He lovingly and perfectly made me. I learned there has been no one like me, there wasn't anyone like me, there will never be anyone like me, and God wanted to have a close relationship with me and LOVE MY SOUL BACK TO LIFE. Frank told me that He was a loving Father, Who loved me unconditionally and immeasurably, like His Son, and They wanted to set me free.

Frank believed I could be set free in prison; this did pique my interest. Frank told me about a Jesus who came to do away with a loveless religion, rules, and regulations like that Pharisaic cult I grew up in. Frank told me about Grace, which means underserved favour. There was nothing I could do to earn my place in Heaven, Jesus had done it all for me. That if I believed in His death on the Cross, His resurrection from the grave, repented and accepted His saving Grace, then God would save me. Consequently, He would see me as if I had lived Jesus' life and Jesus punished as if He had lived my life! I thought this was mean, but Frank said Jesus was God in the form of man, so God was on that cross with Jesus thinking of me. He wanted to breathe new life, His Holy Spirit, into me and bring my soul back to life. Jesus apparently died on the Cross so I didn't have to, to get the sin off me and to expose my value as a Son of God, part of a Royal Priesthood, a Saint (soon to be a Tattooed Saint)! He told me that no matter what I was going through, Jesus had been through worse purposely, so I knew He knew what I was going through. He was with me every day, and even on my worst day, Jesus didn't love me any less. This was not the Jesus, nor the God, whom I had grown up with in the cult.

I was in a spiritual battle and I didn't know it. What I realise now, the reason why my life had become so oppressive is that my battle was not against flesh and blood, it was supernatural. Good and evil had gone to war in the spiritual realm; the prize was my soul for eternity. The reason why I was losing was that I didn't know Jesus in the way I needed to. Unrepented sin and all its effects had darkened my soul and blinded me, so I was lost. I was in a battle I could not win on my own. Frank declared that Jesus could take all the pain, all the guilt, all the suffering away in a moment. Frank left me with this final thought before giving me my first Bible. He said, "When you are alone or at a point of no return, rock bottom; call out the name of Jesus, with all your heart; there is power in the name of Jesus and He will save you." I just nodded my head. Frank then asked if he could pray for me, I nodded again. This time, unlike that time in the courts with the Reverend, I knew Frank meant right there and then, so I was ready. In my desperation, I clung to every utterance. What I later realised, God was speaking through Frank directly to me, penetrating my soul, softening my heart, preparing me. He was right there amid Frank and me. I know this, because when I left Frank, the peace that I felt in that moment quietened my demons. Had they left? Whilst God hadn't left me, I later realised God was showing me that when my focus is on Him, the darkness can't define me. God was also readying me for what was about to happen: old satan's last take-down! Heaven was fighting for me and he was not about to give up. The final battle for my soul was about to take place on landing 3.

When I got back to the landing, I carried on as normal, did my usual rounds, so it wasn't too long before I got the call, "Take this to number 41 NOW!" No sooner had I delivered this to its recipient than I turned around, there was an officer with his arms crossed watching. I had been caught! He looked at me and said, "You are going to come quietly." It wasn't a question; the alternative was to sound the alarm which would alert four others in riot gear. This screw let me step in front of him and led me down to the office. I knew what was coming, I had been here before on the outside when the police tried to interrogate me. When I entered the room, two officers tried to claim they have been watching me do this on several occasions and knew what I had just passed. They claimed it was drugs and started talking about outside courts and 5 years on top of my sentence. They knew I was a first-timer, but I was no longer wet behind the ears. I had learnt to think on my feet, I knew I had nothing illegal on me, and this time it was only a paper message I was transporting. If a search of No.41 took place nothing was incriminating that would be found other than a note, and the worst that could happen to me was to lose my job, which would have been a good thing. I remembered what The Fox shouted, and the Duty Solicitor advised in the Main Bridewell 'no comment'. I didn't grass then, and I was not about to do the same here. They knew they were not getting anything out of me, so they sent me on my way, but left me under no illusion they were out to get me. No sooner had I come out of that room than the demon 'dread' took its opportunity to hop back on board. I was going to die in here…my family was going to die out there. I thought I had cancer… Was I dealing class A drugs again? Was I going to get shivved? Now I was going to get caught and 5 years would be added to my sentence! What was I going to do? I couldn't say no to these dealers, but I couldn't get caught. Next time, it could be heroin.

At this point I'd had enough, I was at rock bottom and suicidal. That night there was heavy, unholy oppression on me, thicker than I had ever known. I was in the darkest place I had ever been. I couldn't see out past the all-consuming dread. I couldn't handle this anymore. I didn't know what to do. Every part of me felt anxious, every ounce of my existence felt lifeless, every cell trembled with fear, and every thought was utterly hopeless.

Then I remembered what Frank said, "Call out His name, it's powerful, and He will save you." I needed to be saved. I waited for my cellmate to fall asleep then under my breath in the dark of my cell, I whispered "Jesus, if you're real, save me…. SAVE ME!" I meant it.

Chapter 43

The day I died in prison

I believed that the prayer I prayed fell on deaf ears. I awoke after an unusually good sleep, got up and got back to my job serving up breakfast. Then I washed down and cleaned up the servery. The movement had begun for those who had jobs or education. In no time at all, the cell doors were closed and locked. This was my signal to head up to landing 3 to pick up the empty food trays. As I was trudging up the stairs by myself again, the dread began to flood my mind. Who was going to call me out and which screw was watching? Momentarily my thoughts were taken to that prayer I prayed last night: what happened or didn't happen? Why did I sleep so well, I began to wonder? I had prayed to God again and meant it, but why didn't He answer? Surely it was the right time. In the midst of these thoughts, I wanted to explore these feelings more, but then the dread stole my last moments. I was now back in the same place emotionally and physically I was when caught by that screw, yards away from the door of that dealer. This was the worst position in the worst place I had ever been. Little did I know it was intentional. You could have got a marker and drawn a white line around my feet, like the outline where a once murdered body lay, and returned 20 years later; and declared right there and then, that was the place of the most terrifying and dreadful moment I ever did experience. The exact place I was caught. I then realised how specific God is, and why when I cried out He didn't turn up immediately. He wanted me to the millimetre in the exact place that I experienced my lowermost emotions, so He could take back the ground in my honour. A place and moment sent from hell, meant to kill, steal and destroy my life would now be the place of my rebirth. Then it hit me....

Every hair on my body stood to attention like angels on parade in God's presence. My skin was like bubble wrap, I had goosebumps all over. Instantly, the atmosphere changed. Was I in another realm? It was no longer oppressive. I could feel an almighty presence which was overwhelming. It felt like the sun had powerfully blown open the roof above and landed on me, only me. I was getting sun-blasted, electrocuted; for a moment I was not in this prison anymore. I knew that above I had an open heaven - it was like the sun shining through a magnifying glass as it concentrates on a single object. I had become the focus of God's pure edifying and perfect love. It was warm, it was safe, and it felt like home. All dread, anxiety, and fear were being burnt away like a piece of gold being purified at 1064 degrees Celsius. All the impurities of my life once lived were expelled from my spirit. Like a vortex, this open heaven consumed every evil emotion and all the hurt and pain was ejected from within me and off me. Like an empty heavenly chalice quivering to be full and filled, the Holy Spirit was released and fell like a deluge, flooding my whole body with God's presence, His love, and peace. It was exaltation that felt like salvation. My mind was blown, the whole universe opened up inside me, and heaven filled me top to bottom, side to side. I was not left guessing what was happening and who was making Himself known to me. It was quite simply Jesus, He was real. I was washed up in His love tornado of pure heavenly emotion. Tears are streaming as I write this, taken back in a moment to the start of my life, my first love when I died and was born again. This was awesome, this was heavenly, this was wonderful, divine, and blissful all at the same time. I was in the worst place I had ever been, feeling the best I had ever known. Higher than I have experienced and not an Ecstasy tablet in sight. Not even 100 pills could take me this high. I was euphoric, ecstatic, and ALIVE! I was lost but now found. I was blind but I could see for the first time. I was healed. I WAS SAVED! This was Amazing Grace; this was PURE LOVE that broke the power of sin and darkness over me. This LOVE so mighty to save, and so much stronger than I could ever imagine or begin to describe. I was being shaken to my core with glorious heavenly thunder. I was left breathless in awe and wonder. This is unfailing love, sent so I could be set free by my King. KING JESUS! I was now standing in a place of victory. He is such a specific God. He is wonderful, and I was changed forever. I knew right there and then I wasn't going to die in this place. Vicki and my Mum - in fact, all my family - would be kept safe. I didn't have cancer and I was no longer alone. I had never been alone, I was simply lost to the fact that Jesus was carrying me all along: the only set of footprints were His. How glorious it felt to be found! How amazing it is to know and be known! How humbling it is to declare I've been saved; I am a son of the living God! As I moved in this holy high picking up those trays, Jesus had made sure no call outs would be made to me that morning, or after. Bless Him forever!

When my family saw me next, they could not fathom what had happened. Of course, they were delighted, but left scratching their heads; almost to the point of wondering, who is this person sitting in front of them? They knew it was me, but wondered if it was good or bad. Had I had a complete and mental breakdown resulting in delirium? For starters, no one can be this happy in jail, and this different, when 14 days prior I was inconsolable and broken. Why was I so different, so radiant, and so positive? I couldn't wait to tell them. I had met Jesus. Now they were sure I had completely lost it! They noted how my whole countenance had changed. On the last visit, I struggled to lift my head or put a sentence together. Now I wouldn't shut up, like the old me, but I was talking clean. I was bouncing, I was on fire. I was excited; it was so hard to contain.

Malcom Carter, the Baptist Prison Minister, confirmed exactly what had happened to me. He was the guy who had set that meeting up with Frank. I needed Frank to know. What should I do next? I also wanted the second opinion of a more informed man of God. Malcom confirmed I had been touched by God and His Perfect Love that casts out all fear, which He poured into me. The reason why the oppression and the darkness had gone: darkness can't exist where there is a great light, and the moment Jesus poured His love onto and into me, the demons vanished. The strength I was now feeling was because He that is *in* me is greater than he (devil) that is in the world. Jesus declared that His sheep heard and obeyed His voice (I am a sheep), and a stranger's voice they no longer follow (satan). I now had a conscience, but it felt good. My soul had been woken up and loved back to life. I was filled with God's Spirit. The essence of who I was created to be had been fathered out of me by the world, so I had been lost in sin, but now I was found and alive in Christ. I had been 'reborn', 'born again'. The old me was dead. I died on that landing without physically dying! At 22 years of age, I was a new creation. I was transformed in the twinkling of eye. Once weak, now strong, full and filled, totally satisfied and more content than I had ever been, even though I was still in jail. But despite where I was, I had quite literally been set free from every negativity, every ounce of guilt, unforgiveness, and pain. For once in my life I could be me, not someone else hiding in plain sight. The new me, the real me, the one that was reborn on that landing, saw heaven put to death that messed-up broken kid who was affected for so long by the cult, by drugs, and by the 3 months of hard jail so far spent. Despite everybody who knew me thinking I was crazy; they could not ignore the fact that I was better. Malcom had taken me through the prayer of salvation, which went something like this:

> "Jesus, I know that I am a sinner, and I ask for Your forgiveness.
> I believe You died for my sins and rose from the dead.
> I turn from my sins and invite You to come into my heart and life.
> I want to trust and follow You as my Lord and Saviour."

God's timing was amazing. No sooner had I been so supernaturally woken up, than I learned I was being relocated to a CAT C prison, HMP Haverigg, in Cumbria. Yes, it was miles away, but I knew from other inmates that it was a holiday camp compared to Walton. I knew right there and then this was God's plan and favour, now I was in *His* camp. Had I left HMP Walton anytime sooner, I would have felt the comfort of my new surroundings and done what most prisoners do when they go to prison: bite their lips, just about get through their sentence and leave in a worse state than when they came in. I reiterate: one of three things happen to inmates when they get sent to jail: they either come out as I have just explained, kill themselves, (which was nearly me), or they call out to Jesus, which was exactly me.

Excitedly, I needed to know exactly what I was dealing with. I needed to know more about this Jesus Who saved me so incredibly and heroically. I started reading the Bible with vigour. The words were coming alive in a powerful way. I now know what some meant when they said 'the Bible is the only book you need the author with you, to help you understand'. God was now living inside of me. His Spirit, I was told, was the same spirit that raised Jesus from the grave. Wow! And He lives in me! What does this mean? I realised I had been resurrected; I had been dead all my life and was now alive, created in the image of God, living in this new identity - This *true* identity - God had always intended. My spirit was born again to live for eternity. I was no longer scared of death, because I knew I would live forever. Yes, of course, this tent that carries my soul will fall apart and one day will no longer work, and it will return to the earth from whence it came. But my born-again spirit is eternal. The Bible says, "Yes, we are of good courage, and we would rather be away from the body and at home with the Lord." (2 Corinthians 5:8 *ESV*) When I close my eyes to this world, I will open them up to God's world, Jesus Christ; the one Who created this world.

I was now excited about what the future would hold, even though I had another 17 months in prison to go. I was ready to tell anyone who cared to know, "Jesus is real!" I was fearless, scared of absolutely nothing. WHAT A TRANSFORMATION!

Chapter 44

Is Jesus real – PROVE IT!

I had just had my first supernatural experience, so I was driven by the need to understand what had happened to me and why was it that Jesus turned up, not Allah or Mohammed, Buddha or Hari Krishna. Doubt had also started to kick in: was it just my imagination? Was I hallucinating even though I had taken no drugs? I was told doubt would pursue me, doubt was a demonic spirit, apparently the devil had just lost his grip over me, and so would be intent on stealing my joy. (John 10:10) 'The thief (devil) comes to steal, kill, and to destroy'. What do you do when all of sudden you are no longer hiding, broken, depressed, suppressed, but now illuminated, different, and then someone asks you what has happened? I could make something up, but my conscience kicked in, the one I never had. Once it was comfortable to lie, but now I had peace for the first time. I couldn't deny Jesus. If I was going to tell people the truth, I needed to be able to respectably present the case for my Saviour. "I have just encountered Jesus and He has set me free." PROVE IT!

A thought! Why is it that when we grow up we stop believing in Santa and all manner of fairy tales, yet there are millions of adults, including some of our finest, including intellects and scientists, highly educated people such as Martin Luther King Jr, Shakespeare, Sir Isaac Newton, Mozart, Charles Dickens, and Nelson Mandela who didn't stop believing in God and Jesus? In the same way, history tells me these men existed.

The fact that I have never seen Mozart doesn't mean he was not real. I was once challenged when I thought 'seeing is believing'. Could I name three of the most powerful things in the world not visible to the naked eye?

1) To touch it can kill you, if your heart stops, it will bring you back to life and it powers almost everything. ELECTRICITY!

2) It can cause tornadoes, create 200-foot waves, blow roofs off houses, and brings up deep-rooted oak trees. WIND!

3) LOVE! But surely you can see love all around, I thought. Name something you love. I said, "My Mum." Prove it! I couldn't. Did this mean the unconditional love I felt so strongly within the depths of my heart was not real? Of course, it was real.

I had learnt a valuable lesson. Seeing is NOT necessarily believing. Dream with me a little more. In the same way, I was led to believe Mozart existed, even though I have never seen him, I learned that there are historical and non-biblical analogues recorded by the Roman 'Tacitus' and Jew 'Josephus', both first-century credible historians, no skin in the game, not Christians, and very much partisan, if not anti-Jesus or at least the idea of the same. Interestingly, both reported factually that a historical Jesus existed; and within 40 years of His death. They also lay claim to witnessing the accounts of His crucifixion. I was left wondering, if only a historical figure, then WHO WAS JESUS? Some say, a great thinker, socialist or philosopher, a prophet even? So many say He's not the Messiah. If true, was this man really crucified for something He was not; The Son of God? We are led to believe He committed no crime and had He simply denounced His Messianic claim He would have been set free. More to the point, if He was not the Son of God, then surely He was completely and utterly 'NUTS'. I struggle to comprehend anything in between, or the messianic rock 'n' roll god complexes, even Charlie Manson delirium or that of Osiris.

Who is Osiris, you may be saying? At best he existed, but unlike Jesus, lacked staying power. Osiris claimed everything Jesus did but apparently did it first, which would arguably make Jesus the copycat. I learned that Christ's coming was foretold throughout the Old Testament many years before both Jesus and Osiris existed. I learned too that over 300 prophecies in the Bible, outline how the Messiah would appear and what He would do. Therefore, it could be argued that anybody could engineer the claim by simply carrying out some of these prophecies.

I was interested in learning the details of these prophecies. (Genesis 3:15) tells us "He will bruise and tread your head underfoot, and you will lie in wait and bruise his heel," meaning there will be one born of a woman who will crush the serpent's head (the devil). It was claimed 'The Son of Man' (Jesus) would defeat satan, the king of this world, by dying on the cross to set His people free both from sin (the influence of satan) and from a death resulting in an eternity without God. This act would save us and restore a right relationship between God and people by removing their sin, as if they never committed it. This didn't make sense to me... Wow! All I must do is believe this and repent of my sins, but moreover, I must believe Jesus is the only way to our loving Creator, Father God. "Sounds extremely bigoted," I thought, "a bit like the cult, if not a bit farfetched; almost that unbelievable it would not be worth making up." Then I thought, if there's a God, there can only be one God, otherwise, He wouldn't be God or worth worshipping. Additionally, why would He create many ways to Him in a world with such order, at least by design? He can't be a God of confusion, otherwise, He would be no God at all. It was a simple revelation: God is singular, and unique: otherwise how can He be God? The concept of many gods or many paths is counter-intuitive.

It's simplicity is its revealing: He either is God and therefore Jesus His Son the only way to Him, or it's a fairy tale, and we may as well crack on with the atheist narrative. Incidentally, a person could not oppose belief in God without the subject of a God in the first place. Some religions have hundreds of gods. Other religions that give credence to one deity, believe their god is distant and they never know if they are going to heaven, so try harder, give more, and hedge their bets. That also didn't make sense to me. If Jesus was really God, He would surely make a way for His people to experience Him, otherwise, He would not be God. "Who created God?" Is a question sometimes heard. The answer to that was easy, "If He needed creating, and then He wouldn't be God." People are created by God, religion is created by man. God didn't create religion, man did, that's why we have so many religions.

Some call Jesus a make-believe crutch for the weak, for those that are scared of the dark. This is presumably as opposed to an atheist, in the dark and scared of the light. I once overheard an interesting debate between a believer and an atheist. The believer ask the atheist, "What is it about the Bible you don't believe?" The atheist said he had never read it. The believer replied, "To be a true atheist you have to be a biblical scholar, in fact, a scholar of all the faiths of the earth, who after a long intellectual journey has concluded there is no God of the universe. You on the other hand, want to circumvent the entire intellectual process and come to the conclusion that there is no God. That's lazy and moronic." Some people actually tell you that apes are your cousins. If you are a Darwinist, you have to accept the conclusion that everything you look at and hold dear is an accident, even those who you love. It's just your DNA, tricking you into survival. There is no love, it can't exist, because love is not molecular; it's just an instinct; it's not even real. If the evolutionists were consistent, then when looking at the sunset over the mountains they would have to say, "Look at that mass gaseous explosion," or "look at that gigantic mound of minerals, dirt and rocks piled upon themselves and crystalized water." Darwinism is all about survival, instinct, no purpose, no value, you are worthless and meaningless and when you die, "who cares?" So why don't we quit throwing those beached whales back into the ocean, surely the whale is trying to evolve? (That was a joke...) More seriously: they take this beautiful creation made by the hands of God Almighty and say it is worthless and meaningless and yet it exists and it works. So, rather than accept it in wonderment, they deconstruct it to see how it accidentally came into being. Really! The more I explored, the more I realised nothing else makes any sense; plus I could feel conviction in my heart to seek out the truth, which is what the Bible lays claim to. (John 8:31-32) "If you abide in my word, you are truly my disciples, and you will know the truth, and the truth will set you free." That reads like a promise, so let's abide, I thought; finish what I started.

Whilst many prophecies could easily be engineered, these are some I simply could not reconcile with the narrative of this being make-believe. The book of (Isaiah 53:3) says, "He was despised and rejected by men, a man of sorrows and familiar with suffering," prophesied 740 years before Jesus was subjected to His ordeal - which He gladly embraced for you and me. How could Jesus determine how or where He would be born, in order to fit in with what was spoken about the coming saviour? As the 'suffering servant' who 'committed no crime' and as 'a man of peace' who the Bible prophesies Messiah to be, why would Jesus of Nazareth choose to compel the authorities to brutalise and crucify Him, just so He could pretend to be 'the One'? Are you scratching your head yet? Try this for size. Psalm (22:16) says, "they will pierce His feet and His hands" - a prophecy written some 300 years before crucifixion even existed. It hadn't been invented. If an impostor were experiencing such torture, the subject would say anything just to stop the pain and get down off that cross, to hell with the people, they don't deserve saving. It's a damn sight worse to stay there and suffer so terribly for a lie…

Instead, the narrative tells us that an innocent man, who had committed no crime, uttered these words through severe pain as His life was leaving His broken and wrecked body, "Father, forgive them for they know not what they do." This seems so profound.

Returning to my thought processes in those early days, I learned the Gospels were written within the same generation of Jesus' death. "Great,"

I thought, "therefore if fabricated, then immediately refutable." But it wasn't, and it stood the test of time despite so many generations with their dictators and detractors going to great lengths to destroy and halt the movement.

"The Bible is either a damn good prank or scam," I thought, a fairy story if you like, "or there is more to it than meets the eye..." As I looked, I learned that this 'fairy tale' is banned in 52 countries, yet Snow White isn't! I wanted to know what made this book different from the many other religions' special books. I learned that everything Jesus did was the opposite to how the founders of other religious movements did things. In the gospel of John, chapter 5 verse 19 tells us that Jesus did only what He saw "the Father doing" and said only what the Father told Him to say, with an outward public display of signs and wonders, witnessed by many, to back it up. There was another remarkable difference I came across: all the other religions were based on earning your place in heaven or paradise based on your works, sacrifice, or keeping ceremonial rules and regulations etc. Even then, you could never be sure of your salvation. It dawned on me how this Jesus-inspired Christianity was the opposite; there is nothing I can do as an individual to save myself and earn my place in the afterlife. Jesus did it all for me on the cross, and when I was saved I was sealed, my destination: Heaven. "Is Christianity even a religion?" I mused. I read about the criminal on the cross next to Jesus. He had clearly not led a good life, full of good works, and probably never lived a religious, ritualistic day in his life; yet Jesus declared, "Today you will be with me in Paradise." Just because he simply believed. So, all you need to do is simply believe and repent? Yes, that is the answer. How is it so? It's to do with GRACE, otherwise known as unmerited and undeserved favour.

Until I experienced the miracle on landing 3, I couldn't understand why 12 normal men who had spent 3 years with Jesus witnessing miracles and knowing He was God in the flesh, went into hiding. It didn't make sense. It was certainly not promoting the Christian Jesus narrative. But what a turn-around! Other than seeing Jesus alive again after His excruciating death, what else could have made them so adamant and such strong proclaimers of the message of "Good News" He carried? When they were once weak and too scared, How were they suddenly filled with joy, boldness and courage? There was no money in it for them; the Roman government and Jewish religious leaders hated them, wanted them destroyed AND eaten alive by animals for sport. They were kicked out of their culture.

Today, there is an average of 140,000 deaths a year of believers who will not denounce their faith. Similar to Jesus on the cross, the disciples then and through the ages until today: They know a truth that no matter the outcome, they will not reject the Saviour of the world. Are they all mad?

Charlie Manson, who claimed to be the Christ of the second coming, surprisingly gave me some clarity. Let's say that within the next 40 years, twelve people claimed Charlie was the Messiah. How credible would their proclamation of faith be and how long do you think his story would last? Two hours? Two days? How about 2 years? Like the gospels, would it last 2000 years and counting? Surely, it would be refuted no sooner than it was publicly announced. This left me wondering… Why didn't the same happen to the gospels? Could they actually be credible accounts? What also interested me was that the four Gospels, Matthew, Mark, Luke, and John, albeit thematic, were all different in their approach. Through their eyes, these were their own honest accounts, unchanged for credibility, not doctored for suitability. Had I found the answer to the question 'who is Jesus'? I was certainly closer. One statement that really left me scratching my head was when Jesus called out from the cross, *"My God, my God, why have you forsaken me?"* (Matt 27:46, *ESV*) This seemed familiar with the cult's God…I wanted to know what this meant. As I researched I learnt that this was the moment the sins of the world, throughout all of time, were cast upon Jesus. He paid the penalty for Humanity which is not only death, but total separation from our Maker. "Ah…" I thought, "that's why Jesus said what He said." He literally experienced Hell so we don't have to! The trump card Jesus pulled out the bag in this moment, was that whilst the powers of Hell thought they were killing the King of Creation, it was actually *they* who were being nailed to that cross! Their power forever broken. Hallelujah!

After all my ponderings, I concluded that I don't think you can be let off calling Jesus just a prophet, socialist, philosopher, or great thinker. He either was The Son of God, or actually a suicidal madman that felt no pain, who hoodwinked the whole world many times over and continues to do the same 2000 years later as a figment of people's imagination. So much so, every hour two believers are murdered because they won't denounce this 'madman' from a fairy tale, whom they have never seen! My question to you would be, have you pursued it for yourself? Isn't it better to have searched and not found, than regretted and cried out "if only"?

Looking aside briefly to the science and evolution narrative, the reason I have always struggled so much with it is summed up in these musings: How did an explosion create such order? If we evolved from the sea crawling on our bellies, how come we decided to stop evolving 6000 years ago? Arguably, science requires more faith than the Bible as it relies on something scientists stipulate happened millions of years ago, when man did not exist. I'm not sure how you can truly measure and observe something you could not truly measure and observe - no one was alive then. Moreover, swear for sure your version above others is the truth and everything else is effectively fiction, or a fairy tale. Some people say the Bible is just a book. I learned it's not one book, it is 66 books and 40 people wrote it over 1500 years. What's more, it contains an unified, consistent message throughout; now that is something.

Talking about the Bible, for hundreds of years, archaeologists have used it to find buildings, historical people and civilizations. It is because of the Bible they have found burial grounds of kings they thought didn't exist. Despite what many people believe, the Bible actually points to historical accuracy. It is an account of real people witnessing real events, who wrote down what they saw. The Jewish people have always been one of the best at this. Perhaps this, along with God knowing they would be the most hated people on the planet, is the reason He chose to clothe Himself as a Jew when He became one of us? Perhaps this is the reason God picked them out above all else to be the nation who would carry the most important message to the world: The message of salvation for all Mankind. When I consider Jesus' words and actions, this would certainly be in keeping with His character.

Some of these people, namely the aforementioned gospel writers, recorded miraculous acts that Jesus performed to prove He was not just a guy talking the talk like everybody else. Some people believed, whilst others couldn't believe their eyes, not open their hearts. But isn't this just how humans are? It's easy to have a logical and intellectual opinion about both science and the Bible, but I don't think you can truly believe one or the other unless you can either time-travel or look into Jesus' claims for yourself and come to a conclusion. (Or unless you experience a supernatural encounter, like me.) The question I found myself left with was, does the supernatural exist? I was sure it did because of what had just happened to me. In a moment, I went from hating God, to knowing and loving God. I experienced heaven and felt the best I had ever been - in the worst place I could ever be in.

The final chapters reveal how this REAL God transformed my life to the point it was unrecognisable, moreover grew me up into faith so I could witness Jesus' miracles amongst us today. Prepare to be amazed, what an adventure, I can't wait to tell you. I have saved the best to last!

Chapter 45

HMP Haverigg, England

Leaving HMP Walton, I was able to return to my civvies, otherwise known as my outside clothes. However, the person climbing into these clothes was not the same person who climbed out of them 3 months prior. 3 months is not a long time, but it is if you have been behind a locked door for most of it. It was a rare treat to get to see Liverpool again from the coach that was transporting me to the Lake District, Millom, and HMP Haverigg. I was excited, knowing I was going to a new jail because of the barbaric one I had left. It took two hours to get from Liverpool to Millom. I knew I was nearing our new destination as the concrete jungle was replaced by the motorway and then the countryside. The deeper the coach travelled, the larger the mounds of the earth grew up out of the ground: hills were everywhere. It was in the middle of nowhere on my way to somewhere I have never been to before. I can't overstate what a thrill it was to see the outside world again, particularly the countryside in all this splendour: God's creation experienced through virtuous eyes. Strangely, it took me back to the train going on my first holiday when I left the cult. If you have ever watched programs like Big Brother and Celebrity Get Me Out Of Here, some of the contestants are broken within weeks of being taken out of their comfort zone. A need in them is so strong it is no longer met by their circumstances. They suffer a breakdown, and want to go home. I can't overstate how oppressive HMP Walton was, which made this journey through God's wonderful countryside eminently more pleasurable. It felt like an escape.

I arrived, greeted by the usual yellow mesh fence, and a sign that said Welcome to HMP Haverigg. It looked like a prison, but where was the prison building, like that I saw towering out of the Liverpool earth over the 30-foot fence when arriving at Walton? I soon realised all the buildings were single-storey. After 3 months of being locked up by another, I now had my own key, which made this place feel like Disneyland compared to the coffin I left at Liverpool. Who would've thought I could get that excited by a key? Although this wasn't freedom, it felt like one step closer to home. The only door that was locked was the front door of the billet, from 8 p.m. until 7 in the morning. This key was for my cell. It would be me locking my door each night.
I soon swapped my clothes over, changing back into the usual prison attire. Dressing like a freeman was short-lived and felt cruel, because momentarily I was able to imagine my release day. This time, it was easier to give my clothes away to the prison lock-up. I had a bounce in my stride: I was saved, fearless, and I had escaped the place that wanted to take my life. God's timing was so perfect: I felt blessed, even though I remained in prison. This new place didn't feel like a jail.

We were heading to the induction billet, but not before we passed through "Beirut". These the rundown billets to which we would go after induction. Haverigg Prison is built on the site of an old RAF airfield training centre opened in 1967. The billets in Beirut were the original RAF digs, so they were old. When we arrived, the darkness of the night was falling: it was super-cold. One of the first things I noted was that there was a hill behind us that was covered in snow. It was still winter, so the air was fresh and crisp. I was blowing out steam like a baby dragon, as the hot air from my lungs mixed with the cold air of the countryside. I now had a donkey jacket that went down to my knees, with blue padding in the shoulders. I had prison-issue boots, which were so much better than the brown plastic dancing shoes I had in Walton. These boots looked a little bit like old-fashioned football boots, but without the studs. I was thankful for that coat because this place was freezing: even the brass monkeys had Berghaus's on! This prison looked like the place where I stayed on my first school trip to North Wales! It had a working farm, so the smell of animal manure was distinct, and we weren't too far from Sellafield, but Molasses Mo was now a very distant memory: there was no chance he was here. Every 10 or 20 steps, a manhole cover would spit out steam, a bit like the sidewalks in New York. These manholes were releasing enormous amounts of billowing white mist. My first reaction was, "Is that going to explode?" The guiding officer commented, "Don't worry, it's just the prison blowing off a little steam. Don't be afraid, it's not dirty smoke. It is, however, very hot, so do not go too close." This place was oil and steam-fuelled.

When we landed in the induction block, it was a jail within a jail, newly built. It was segregated from the rest of the prison. Were we being quarantined? Within the compound, there was a games and movie room, a small education block with a library, and of course the billet we were about to step into. I was one of four who travelled up from Liverpool. We were the last ones to arrive and there were four rooms left. It didn't really matter which one we got, as they were all the same. This time I was not two'ed up. It was quite a sweet deal: I had my own key, my own room, some solitude, I could come and go as I wanted within the billet, watch telly, sit off in another's pad, or lock myself behind the door. There were 16 of us on the billet. We shared a television room and a small kitchen. Although not as memorable as the first time when I left the cult, I got to watch television again regularly. Of course, we watched what the general consensus agreed to, which was fine. It reminded me of that 10-year-old Kevin leaving the cult: I watched and enjoyed anything that the TV wanted to spit out. Most of my new neighbours seemed suitable enough; there didn't seem to be any with a negative temperament, at least towards me; apart from one. He was in the middle of coming off heroin, also known as cold turkey. This phrase is attributed to the goose bumps that occur with abrupt withdrawal from opioids, and resembles the skin of a plucked refrigerated turkey. Several of us were sat in his cell and he passed that devil pipe to me for my turn, but I was now a Jesus freak so I passed it to the next person. No sooner had he wrapped his lips around that rolled foil, reheated the brown-like ladybird on the top of the other piece of foil, than he was releasing steam, like the manhole covers we just passed. Rather like a dragon, the one he was chasing around his foil, he caught it and sucked up the chemically infused cloud; his lungs inflated, his veins the magnet to the poison. It refuelled his brain and nervous system and he was brought back to life, at least compared to his previous state. He was no longer cold, the turkey was hot, in fact, it was no more. You could see him being released from the cage he had been rattling in. All the colour came back to his face, he put his head back and closed his eyes. What was bizarre was that he carried on interacting, wanting to enter into deep and full-scale conversations, all the while with his eyes almost closed as he looked at you through the sliver between his eyelids.

Everybody in this billet had come from a much more oppressive place. We were all glad to be there, so the whole week felt like we were holidaying. When I moved to Beirut I was living in a glorified shed. I had the freedom of this village, so I could walk the grounds freely. The whole prison was broken up into the reception, the block, 'Beirut', and an area like the induction block with 12 billets. Each inmate had to earn their stripes before they could be considered for the upper block and leave Beirut. It took two months of waiting for my promotion. When we moved to our final destination, it seemed the screws liked to keep Mancs with Mancs, Cumbrians with Cumbrians; so naturally, I ended up with the Scousers. It was pleasant, and it had that holiday camp feel like the induction block. This was a relief as it would be the place I would see out the last 14 months of my sentence. It was only one Christmas, but two summers, so it still felt a long way off. Nevertheless, I had cleared my first hurdle, the 6-month mark. The next hurdle was the halfway point. Once I had broken the back of my sentence, it was all downhill thereon in a good way.
I remember one particular visit from a friend at this jail, A.K.A The

Surgeon, aptly named because he was a real brain surgeon. He was born with a silver spoon in his mouth, a significant career path and I suspect was paid a salary some can only dream of. Why would he risk everything!? The Surgeon was a thoroughly decent chap, and the fact he also had access to medical cocaine meant he was good company too. As he moved in our circles when required he would be on call if a member of the firm he represented had been knifed or had taken a bullet. Shockingly, he eventually became an illegal chemist and started manufacturing amphetamine. But this was not the odd gram or kilo, this was production on a huge scale. The Surgeon would visit me in Haverigg and bring my Dad. When details of his trial hit the press, it was reported how he would visit known felons, drug dealers in prison, me. This did make me chuckle as Dad was none the wiser. Surely, he was thought of as a suspect. If the police ran Dad through their computers, they would have found him in possession of his own criminal record with a son in jail for drug dealing now driving shotgun with a major amphetamine manufacturer, who was the doctor to the underworld. Did they think my Dad was a big time Charlie Potato, we did chuckle about it together some years later. The Surgeon ended up getting 14 years. What a waste of all that education and privilege. No longer a brain surgeon, he was writing to me from prison instead of visiting me. How crime can create such a level playing field. Me an autistic mouth breather, my friend a brain surgeon, both convicted drug dealers surviving in our 7 ft by 7 ft brick walled coffins.

Weekends within my new home would always be interesting. Most on the upper block were deemed to be more responsible, so many were getting home leave, which was increasing the number of drugs smuggled into the prison. It would be party time, usually lots of Ecstasy and weed. As tempting as it was to partake, I was now a Christian, and the desire to be off my head was less. There was a new Governor who wanted to crack down on the free flow of drugs, so home leave became no longer a right. These officers were not stupid; they knew who the movers and shakers were. Inmates were getting moved around left, right and centre and if you were thought to be a drug user, particularly a dealer, you would be 'Shanghaied'. This meant they came for you when least expected, usually in the middle of the night, taking the inmate against his will and shipping them off back to a CAT B jail. My billet soon became the destination for long-termers, which meant anyone with a sentence of three years or more. This meant that all the lifers, ended up as my neighbours. Surrounded by and sleeping under the same roof as murderers was surreal. They included an axe murderer, a contract killer, with several more sinister inmates who you knew little about. This led me to believe what they did was very depraved; however, by this time they had been inoculated to their past. They were very institutionalised and kept themselves to themselves. Yet another season in the life of Kevin, but one that was the beginning of the end. It would soon be 1996, the year of my release. Bring it on!

Chapter 46

Retained by the police again

My first job in HMP Haverigg paid £7 a week, but it was soul-destroying. I was connecting plugs to chains, the very same you would find in your bathtubs. Due to good behaviour and time served, next, I was able to apply for a job in the kitchens. This was the best-paid job in the prison at £14 a week, and other than mealtimes the day was my own. All I had to do was clear the dining hall after each meal three times a day. In this place, we all ate meals together. This was the easiest most sought-after job in the prison, but as soon as a church orderly job became available, I was on it. So what if it only paid £7 a week, and it meant evening work? I didn't care, because I was on fire for Jesus, and this seemed like destiny. I didn't make any secret of the fact that I was a Christian, which is a testimony in itself to the transformation that had taken place in my life. Being a Christian is nothing to boast about in prison: it's seen as a sign of weakness. Little did the inmates know that I was stronger than I had ever been! Regardless, most of the inmates would keep me at arm's length, which meant I was sometimes the target of some playground abuse, and attempts at humiliation, but I didn't care. I was impenetrable and full of God's strength. Strangely, like with Mad Roy, God placed some real tough gangsters in my life who were from Liverpool, who took me under their wing to protect me. Mad Dog so-and-so was one: for obvious reasons, I won't name him. This was a guy not to be messed with. He was known as one of the hardest men in Liverpool, and was doing time for kidnap and shoving a pen into the ear of his victim. He was also a well-trained martial artist, built like a tank, and scared everyone apart from me because he had my back. Well...actually, he did scare me a little! Unfortunately, several years after his release, he was shot dead in Liverpool. The second guy was the funniest Scouser I ever did know; he was known only as Joey. This guy had been inside for years, not because his crime was really serious, armed robbery I recall, but he kept getting time added to his sentence because he was absolutely nuts and uncontrollable. He, like Mad Dog, wanted to take care of me. Joey always had things others didn't have, such as a games console which he would lend to me for a few days each week. Always, he would pop his head into my room and say, "You all right lad, no-one bothering you?" Both these guys ran the jail during their time with regards to drugs etc, so, naturally, it came to an abrupt end and they were both shanghaied. I look back and find it absolutely bizarre that they treated me like they did. I can only credit God's favour and protection. As true as that is, I do remember a time in Walton when a complete stranger approached me with a message from Mr Big and those above him, to thank me personally on their behalf for not throwing them under the bus. Maybe Mad Dog and Joey knew more about me than they let on. Everybody knew everybody's business.

Christmas time was as memorable as the last, but this time for the right reason. It was in prison and of course, I missed spending it with my family, but I knew it would be my last Christmas behind bars. When New Year came, it was celebrated like no other I can remember before or since, at least without drugs. It was 1996! I was going home this year and I had six months left! With three months to go, I was offered the chance to take home leave. The chance to experience freedom for three days was way too alluring but gave no problems. However, when I returned, time dragged like it did in HMP Walton. This is going to sound weird, but I was glad to be back in prison. It was amazing to see my family and spend time with Vicki. I also went to visit the Bumper in jail. He had been through it like me, losing the top of his ear in a fight. I remember on the last night of my home leave we all went for a family meal. I was so spent, I had aches in my joints and couldn't stand for long periods. It had all been too much all at once. I was mentally and physically drained. Frank agreed to take me back to prison, what a guy! He is my inspiration and why I have gone back to prison to carry on the work he started, and imparted, to me.

The weeks leading up to my taste of complete freedom I remember fondly. It was the summer, more particularly The Euros 1996. These European Football Championships were held in England, remembered by how Gazza scored that goal against Scotland when he flipped it over the head of the defender and in one movement volleyed it into the back of the net. The night of the semi-final England v Germany, was the eve of my release. We were beaten as per usual on penalties, but you could not alter my mood. The following day it was all over and I would be free forever. I can safely say that this night I was the most excited I had ever been in all my life. At 9 o'clock the following morning it was over. Vicki couldn't pick me up, so Dave and my Dad did. Walking out of that place was just awesome, although with some sadness because I had met some really decent people, some great Christians, some inspiring people, and I had been on one of the greatest adventures of my life. Despite the speed of this chapter, my last 17 months in HMP Haverigg did drag but was a breeze compared to Walton. I can quite honestly say that if I could live my life again, I would NOT change a thing. An experience that should have made me bitter, actually made me better, and laid the foundation of who I became and who I am today. Without my lowermost point on that landing in HMP Walton, I may never have got to experience heaven on earth and meet Jesus supernaturally in this life. Thankfully, He wasn't finished with me yet…!

Being home for good was amazing! My parents were back together again, the new house now felt like home, and I was so in love with Vicki. Absence from the one you love absolutely wrecks your heart, but in a good way, especially once reunited. It was great to see all the lads again. I had some great nights in some of the old haunts: the places I used to go to get off my head, but I didn't take drugs anymore. The point is, I didn't need to be off my head anymore. I had nothing I needed to escape from, and I didn't want to dishonour this wonderful second chance Jesus had given me. There were times when temptation pulled hard on my will-power but I was strong and by His grace I resisted. I took confidence from what I overcame; they were little spiritual battles that were edifying and strengthening me. They were also evidence that I had changed. I was growing up into Jesus, into my identity, and into my destiny, the plan God had called me to. I had received a 40-month sentence but completed only half in jail. The other half would be 'out on licence', which is quite precarious as any criminal activity that carried the ability to be prosecuted would result in being sent back to do the other 20 months. Drunk and disorderly, aggressive behaviour, even if only slightly injuring another, not turning up to my probation appointments, not doing what my probation officer told me to do; any of these, or similar occurrences, would have sent me back to prison.

I was told by my probation officer to return to education. Remember that kid, the one that struggled throughout school and only had five GCSEs because he cheated? Consequently now, I do not lay claim to passing those GCSEs. I was now being urged to go to an open day for adult education. When I attended, I soon realised that if I could be educated to a professional level, an employer wouldn't be left wondering if I had a past. The fact that I was an ex-gangster drug dealer, user, and abuser who went to jail, would be the last thing they would think. I decided to step out in faith. When I learned that John Moores University offered the opportunity to start a HND course in construction, I was willing to make a fool of myself. I was told this would fast-track me on to a degree. I didn't need any qualifications, as I could be admitted as a mature student, which is 21 and over, and I was 24. Obviously, there was some trepidation, as I believed I was still incapable of being educated at any level, never mind degree level. I didn't realise who I had become and that what God says in the Bible was about to come true.

'Therefore, if anyone is in Christ [that is, grafted in, joined to Him by faith in Him as Saviour], he is a new creature [reborn and renewed by the Holy Spirit]; the old things [the previous moral and spiritual condition] have passed away. Behold, new things have come [because spiritual awakening brings a new life].' (2 Corinthians 5:17, *AMP.*)

I had a new life! I was a new creation, about to experience this verse in its fullest sense. After a year, I successfully achieved a sufficient pass to transfer on to a degree course. This is clear proof that God is in the game of transformation, and how He can take a broken life and change it so irrevocably. By the second year of my degree course, I was the highest achieving student in the main syllabus, Valuation and Law. YES, LAW! There was a special award ceremony. I won a panoramic digital camera and a year's free film. At this special presentation, Mum could not have been any prouder of me. I was starting to pay back her faith in me. This is how amazing my God is. I was flying! Within three years, I had graduated with honours. Two years after graduating and at my first attempt, I qualified as a Chartered Surveyor. From "at Her Majesty's Pleasure", now "in Her Majesty's service": a member of her Royal Institute of Chartered Surveyors. Once known as Kevin Cockburn FN3698, now I have worthwhile letters after my name **'Kevin Cockburn BSC (Hons) MRICS'.**

But God wasn't finished there…

My secretary… Wait there, let me say that again, "my secretary;" little old me had a secretary. On this particular day, she called through to me. "I've got Merseyside Police on the phone." Naturally, I was taken aback. The last time I spoke to them I was in the Main Bridewell. I reluctantly asked, "What's it regarding?" Then my secretary uttered the following, "It's to do with The Main Bridewell." Can you imagine? For a moment I thought, "It's a prank;" but no one in my industry, least of all my secretary, knew I had been an ex-resident of this jail. I took the call to control the conversation, because it was either one of the lads, like the Bumper, getting me back for, "Is Charlie White available," or it really was the police, which worried me even more. But…in the past, I had been retained by the police as a criminal; now the police wanted to retain me again, but in a professional capacity! The jail had been dormant since it was condemned and they wanted my advice; not only on its value or how to sell it, but if I could sell it for them! You could have knocked me over with a feather, particularly when they told me to come to their office and pick up the keys! I was given the keys to every door and front door to the jail I had been in 10 years before! The very same keys that locked me up. I later realised this was symbolic. God was giving me back the keys that locked me up, sending me back into prison so that through me He could set others free, like Frank had done for me. The Main Bridewell is a hotel now, which was exactly what I said it would become. What a sense of humour God has. WOW WOW WOW! See below verbatim the article from the Liverpool Echo. Google my name and the Main Bridewell, and you can view the actual article yourself.

"The former prison, situated in Cheapside behind the city's magistrate's courts, is Grade II listed and property agent Kevin Cockburn, of Dears Brack, is marketing it on behalf of Merseyside Police.

However, as it stands at the moment, the current interior is described as only "severely functional with absolute minimum decoration".

Mr Cockburn is inviting offers for a sealed bid tendering process with the price tag expected to be in excess of £600,000.

Yesterday he told the Daily Post that whoever takes the building will face a challenge.

He added: "It is not just the building as a whole that is listed, but every part inside is too; so although the planners have accepted that some changes would have to be made for conversion, they would not allow any substantial alterations.

"We expect the deal would suit a developer with an entrepreneurial spirit who might want to create something a bit different. It is possible it could be converted into apartments. There is a concept that has appeared elsewhere in the UK called the crash pad. With Capital of Culture now getting nearer, it could even be turned into a themed hotel, catering for people who fancy the idea of being banged-up for the night.

"The structure of the building, which was built between 1860 and 1864, is of solid brick with vaulted corridors. It has a total floor area of just under 20,000 sq ft, and has 47 cells."

If the above is not evidence enough of a real God and how one life, when submitted to His grace, power and provision can become so radically changed, then you are beyond convincing. In reality, the transformation from a messed-up kid, drug user, seller, and convict, to what I became, is only part of the real transformation. Remember, I was brought up in a cult, whose god I thought was the only God, the same I confused with the real God. In fact, I can now say, hand on my heart, I forgive everyone who has ever hurt me or offended me; more particularly those in that cult. If you're still in doubt as to the authenticity of my transformation and whether God and Jesus are real. Let me have one more go. The Bible says that signs and wonders follow those that believe: my final chapters are about the supernatural.

Chapter 47

Returning to prison – Mr Big

In 2014, I was heading back into jail as a freeman, on fire for Jesus. I was invited to participate in a course about reoffending behaviour with a focus on restorative justice.

I was nervous about returning to prison. The first was to visit my Dad, the second was to serve time and now the third was to make amends. Interestingly, my life also can be broken up into three parts. Born into a cult, reborn into the world, and then born again on the landing at HMP Walton. It seemed obvious that I should return to jail, as Jesus had me return to the place of my lowermost experience to save me. What was I saved from? An eternity without God. Why was I saved? To secure my eternity and right-standing with God. In short, I was also saved to save. Despite the obvious, I needed further affirmation. Two significant things would happen on this day. The first, the Prison Chaplain Shawn prophesied there was a book in me; that's come true. The second simply blew my mind, and this is what happened.

I could have gone back on any other day and to any other prison at any other time, but God chose this time, as this day was predestined - set in motion in 1993, when I started selling drugs. Immediately, I recognised a face from my past; but not enough to have the confidence to go and reintroduce myself. Then he clocked me. He was a chunky guy and certainly looked like he could handle himself. As he walked past, he paused, recognising me; but the penny had not quite dropped.

There was an uncomfortable silence, which I broke when I burst out, "Did you use to be a doorman in that club?" (The one I was arrested in). He said, "Yeah, how come I remember you?" I said, "Do you remember so-and-so?" I was referring to Mr Big. He said, "Yes!" Now he was intrigued because he wanted to know how I knew Mr Big, which momentarily put him on his guard. I quickly proclaimed, "I was one of his boys." He said, "No way! Mr Big is my best mate and when I got married, he was my best man." I hadn't spoken to Mr Big since the night I was arrested; some 20 years had passed since then. This excited me straight away because I knew that when he saw Mr Big again, I would quite naturally come in the conversation and Mr Big would be told I was a Christian returning to jail. I thought "Great, that seed will be planted, someone will water it and God will bring the increase." I was believing in Mr Big's salvation. It would surely intrigue Mr Big when he spoke to his bezzie as to why on earth I was back in jail, as he had only ever known me as a drug user, abuser, stedhead, and a dealer; certainly not a Christian.

My mind was totally blown. It was the last week of this course, week 6, which is where the inmates get to show, by way of an act of restitution, how they are sorry for the crime they committed. The inmate would stand up in front of family and all the other inmates and effectively repent and, by way of a token gesture, give something back. Some will write a letter to their victim, others will draw something like the word "Sorry", or make something; all manner of things would be declared and offered up. It was Mr Big's bezzies turn to step up. He had written a poem. The content went along the lines of, I paraphrase, "I thought I was a big man, I thought I did big things, but when I came to prison, I hid and pretended I was still a big man, but inside I was breaking apart, and then Jesus turned up and changed my life forever." WOW! I nearly fell off my chair. Two things: if I wasn't sure, I now knew that this is the exact place I need to be regularly for the rest of my life. Secondly, but more importantly, it would only be a matter of time before Mr Big was going to know what his bezzie knew, what I knew,

Jesus is real! I marvelled at how God was working things out 20 years ago, "aligning the stars" so that He could touch Mr Big, through his bezzie, endorsed further by meeting me. I believe if he hasn't already, it will only be a matter of time before Mr Big meets his King!

Talking of bezzies, remember that chapter about how I met Jockstrap Dave? Dave and I didn't know how we went from being head-to-head ready to fight to become bezzies, still close today. I threw a request upstairs; this is what God revealed. Chris, Dave's mum, was anti-drugs. I expected her to shun me when I was arrested, but she would write to me in prison wonderful letters of great encouragement, which I didn't deserve. When I was released, I saw Dave less, but I still made time to go and see his mum and catch up over a cup of tea. I remember one outstanding day. I hadn't seen Chris for a while, and God had put something on my heart to go and see her that day, so I did. I had seen her many times before, but this time she opened up a conversation about a clairvoyant on the radio, who had revealed something that moved Chris. Let's be clear here; I believe this one is real, although some are fake. The reason why a stranger can recall things about another from the afterlife, is because a demonic entity from the spirit world is giving the revelation; and the spirit world is outside of time. Although it cannot read your mind, it can certainly influence your thought life. It knows who you lost, your loved ones, your desires, and your concerns, often because that dark spirit puts the fear of the same in you. The devil's aim of clairvoyance is simply to keep you reassured about your future, so you don't feel the need to go to the real source of comfort, who is Jesus. One of the last things Jesus said on this earth was, "I must go, so that the comforter can come: the Holy Spirit." (John 16:7) The point of this story is: this was the first time Chris opened up, which allowed me to share my faith. We had our deepest conversation ever about it. Soon after, Chris sadly died. That last chat over a cup of tea was preordained. It was no coincidence. God was using me, somehow in readiness, because He would soon take her home. How God turns things around! For over 20 years, Dave would go to town on me regarding my faith, trying to pull it apart. Not in a bad way - it was his way of searching for the truth I claimed I had. He wanted me to talk him into it, but always had a comeback to any suggestion I made. A person is not reached and saved through a convincing argument... It's through faith, which of course comes through hearing the Word of God. It also comes from being chosen and drawn by the Holy Spirit, if only the object of Jesus' affection (you) would submit.

After 20 years, we were going around in circles. He had nothing new, and I had no more to add. Some 12 years after his mum had passed, Dave and I experienced the manifest presence of God in a boozer and Dave gave his life to Jesus. It was simply amazing! At this moment, God revealed exactly what I always had faith to believe and Dave hoped for: that his mum was safe and sound with Him in Heaven. Moreover, because this was so powerful and undeniable, now heaven was Dave's destination! Something he repelled for so long.

One-touch from God in one second can change everything. If you have a friend or loved one that doesn't know Jesus, never give up on them. It was a privilege to breathe the same air as Chris, matched by the wonderful gesture to become part of her family, even if for one day only when they invited me to sit alongside them in the funeral cortege to see her off. One of Chris's favourite songs was one of mine, and it was played at her funeral: INXS 'Never Tear Us Apart'. I look forward to the day I see you again, Chris. You are and will always be part of the very fabric of my life. I love and honour you in every way I possibly can, which I suspect could not be better than being the person that God used to lead her son, one of my bezzies, to Him, and ensure his eternity is with his mum in heaven. Wow! How things can come around full circle!

Chapter 48

A life turned around!

Sadly, we have come to the end of this adventure. The only way to finish this book is to proclaim what God has done in my life as a free man now ministering in prison. The chance to share what happened to me and how Jesus could do the same for them. I have experienced signs and wonders. I have seen dry bones come to life. I have seen broken lives set free. There is nothing like co-labouring with God and seeing inmates, the lost, experience their heavenly Father for the first time when the presence and love of the Almighty shines into a life.

I would always highlight the fact there are 66 books in the Bible. The first five were penned by Moses who was a murderer. Most of the Psalms were written by David who was a murderer and adulterer. Solomon wrote two books of the Bible, but in the last years of his life, he went after foreign gods. Paul, (originally named Saul), wrote 13 books of the Bible and was responsible for the stoning of hundreds of Christians before his conversion. When a Christian was stoned, it was to death. Four of the epistles were written by Paul. From where? You've guessed it: Prison. The writer of the book of James was Jesus's half-brother. He grew up in the same house as Jesus, but didn't believe in Him as the Son of God until after His resurrection. Then there's Peter, who wrote at least two books of the New Testament. He denied Christ three times, but ended up becoming the leader of the early Church! If you rip out all the books of the Bible written by murderers and failures, you would lose most of the New Testament and much of the Old. Their teachings are read by millions. Just because someone failed in life doesn't mean that they aren't deserving of honour. More particularly, prisoners' futures do not have to be defined by their pasts. Those that have been forgiven much, love much. Jesus definitely wants broken messed-up people, because they will display the greatest transformation.

When confronting convicts, I declare Jesus can do for them what He did for me. I usually get one of the following responses: humoured, sometimes laughed at; told to do one; and then, occasionally, a listener will want to know more. My job is to plant the seed and have faith another will water it, and God will bring the growth. This is true; but do we sometimes use the same as an excuse to play it safe?

God's Spirit highlighted to me about His power that is within me. As with every reborn believer, He wanted to use me more powerfully: in particular, to display His supernatural signs and wonders, as Jesus said those who follow Him would. He gave me a revelation about Peter and the storm, detailed in the verse from The New Testament set out below:

"Immediately He directed the disciples to get into the boat and go ahead of Him to the other side [of the Sea of Galilee], while He sent the crowds away. After He had dismissed the crowds, He went up on the mountain by Himself to pray. When it was evening, He was there alone. And in the fourth watch of the night (3:00-6:00 a.m.) Jesus came to them, walking on the sea. When the disciples saw Him walking on the sea, they were terrified, and said, "It is a ghost!" And they cried out in fear. But immediately He spoke to them, saying, "Take courage, it is I! Do not be afraid!" Peter replied to Him, "Lord, if it is [really] You, command me to come to You on the water." He said, "Come!" So, Peter got out of the boat, and walked on the water and came toward Jesus. But when he saw [the effects of] the wind, he was frightened, and he began to sink, and he cried out, "Lord, save me!" Immediately Jesus extended His hand and caught him, saying to him, "O you of little faith, why did you doubt?"
(Matthew 14:22-23, 25:31, AMP)

The revelation was, "faith is spelt R.I.S.K." I was about to learn what it meant. When the storm arose, only one disciple experienced a miracle first-hand. Note that Peter effectively asked if he could get out of the boat into the very storm he was scared of, and walk on it. Just think about that for a moment. I can imagine when Jesus said "Come" he panicked, hoping Jesus would say "no." Perhaps he hoped that Jesus would come to him first or at the very least calm the storm. But Peter was invited to walk on stormy water to reach Jesus. The Bible tells us that Peter began to sink only when he took his focus off Jesus. The essence of this story is to stay focused on Jesus and you won't be defined by the storms in your life.

What excited me more and the most was my understanding that R.I.S.K. = Miracle. Peter walked on water because he took the *risk* to step into the storm, whilst the other disciples clung to the perceived comfort of the boat. They witnessed the miracle that Peter experienced. I decided right there and then I didn't want to be like the boat-clinging disciples anymore, in the perceived comfort and safety of the boat. I wanted to experience a miracle but knew I had to step out of my boat first, figuratively speaking.

I made an inward declaration, and the next time I was in prison, I chose the meanest looking scariest inmate and told him about Jesus. To say I chose well was an understatement. This is how it went…, "I've been where you've been, Jesus saved me, turned my life around…." No sooner had I mentioned Jesus than he stopped me in my tracks. As expected, he didn't want to know anymore, nor did he want to be pushed on the topic. He was categorical. "I don't believe in God!" His tone told me to move on. Ordinarily, I would step away and recline back into my boat, safe in the knowledge I've shared and planted the seed, over to you Jesus. But this time, I was determined to get uncomfortable. I was going to get out of that boat, step onto the water and take that risk. All the while, I was doing my duck impression, calm on the outside and paddling like there's no tomorrow underneath. I began to speak without knowing the words I would say. When I opened my mouth in faith, I was offering up my tongue as a landing strip for the Holy Spirit to minister through me, with me, for me, and to the person in front of me. Instantly, words, more particularly scripture, fell out of my mouth. I knew God had turned up. He was always there; He was just making himself known, and it went something like this…

"Well, you may not be interested in God, but God is interested in you. He pursues you all your life. He chooses a moment like this, for a time like this. He's right here, right now, and wants to make Himself known to you. Jesus loves you, knew you before the world began, predestined you for greatness and He wants to touch your heart right now." Remember, faith comes by hearing and hearing the Word of God. I was speaking the Word of God over him; the demons oppressing the spiritual environment hate the Word of God. So they have to disappear. Then I mentioned that the Bible clearly states that, "In the last days, God will pour His Spirit out on all flesh." At this point, I looked this guy square in the eye and said, "If God was here wouldn't you want to meet Him, to experience Him?" He said, "Well erm…..yes!" FAITH! I asked, "Could I lay my hand on you?" He agreed. I asked God to pour out His Holy Spirit, and watched in awe as God's love and presence were released. This guy was now in shock, his whole countenance changed. He said in wonder, "What's going on?" I said, "More, Lord," which is exactly what happened! I was more shocked than the guy who was getting touched by God! This inmate's scowl had turned into a smile and his face expressed what he was now feeling: amazement, awe, and wonder. I didn't know what to do at that moment. It was only broken by the need to return to the session. Before we returned, I explained, "God is wooing you, He loves you, He always has and He wants to set you free; and He just proved how real He is." I couldn't wait for the following week to see him again. I was sure he would have experienced more of Jesus, in dreams, maybe even like I did that day on that landing. When he arrived the following week, he went straight into the Chapel. The sessions are held in the world faith room, where he should have gone. I expected him to start waxing lyrical about the goodness of God, but he had just experienced the worst week he had ever had. Then I realised, of course, the devil knew he was about to lose him, so he was under demonic oppression. The aim was to keep him from returning to me, more particularly to this moment we were about to have. I said, "Why have you come into the Chapel?" He said, "I needed to and wanted to pray for my family." I must admit that I did get a little bit of an ego trip when I laid hands on him the week before and God turned up, but I was about to be taught a lesson in humility. In the middle of this conversation, this guy stopped in his tracks, I hadn't laid a hand on him or called down heaven. He just looked at me in shock and said, "It's happening again!" I said, "What?" He continued, "The same as last week." That's me put in my place. But I knew what God was doing. He was inviting this guy into a relationship with Him. So I said exactly that. "Now you know God is real, do you want to experience the same for the rest of your life?" He answered, "Yes". Then we went through the prayer of salvation; he gave his life to Jesus and invited the Holy Spirit to fill him and take residence. I had just done what Jesus said we would do, which was to continue the works of Jesus and do greater things. I had just seen a dead man die to self and be born again, changed inside and out by one touch from God. I then realised how much of a privilege and blessing it is to be used to lead another to their salvation because I get to experience the presence and power of God as much as the love-subject God is wooing through me and around me.

Off the back of this miracle, I was "Godfident", like a dog with a bone. In that 6-week course, I got to experience the same thing with six other inmates, all of whom gave their lives to God. One particular guy was in for brutally attacking another who pulled a knife on him. He blamed the knife attacker for his own being in jail, which is understandable, as it was self-protection. This guy looked at me and said, "something in me has changed, and for the first time since my crime I realised I had now forgiven my attacker." I looked at him and asked, "Do you know why?" He didn't. I said, "God is touching your heart and softening it. He wants to set you free from all unforgiveness, and He's right here, right now, and loves you…"

This guy started to get tearful as God began touching him. You just don't do this so openly in jail! In an attempt to comfort the new guy, I turned to point to the guy from the first week to say, "Don't worry, he got what your experiencing 5 weeks ago." What was quite funny - but amazing - was that as I turned to him, he wasn't with us anymore. He had fallen back in his chair with his head all the way back, under the presence of God! I said, "Are you alright?" He opened one eye, and out the side of his mouth in the thickest Scouse accent, the said, "This is like meditation, lad." Like the guy deep in God's presence, the new guy in front of me gave his life to Jesus.

I will finish with this. Mid-course, one of the questions we ask concerns something Jesus declares (Luke 19): "Why did Jesus say, 'Salvation has come to this house'?" On one occasion, there was a Muslim on this course who blurted out, "Because He was the Son of God." Now, Muslims do not believe this; they believe Jesus is only a prophet. I had to wait until the session was over before I took up this statement with him. Because he was Muslim, I had already increased the risk because he already had a faith. But I wanted to increase the risk more. There were four sitting around the table. I seized the moment and reminded the Muslim what he had said. I declared, "flesh and blood did not reveal that to you." I then broke into the usual, "God's right here, Jesus loves you. And He is the Son of God. Can I lay my hand on you? Holy Spirit, come." This man was now sliding down the back of his chair under the presence of God. No sooner had he pulled himself together, than he gave his life to Jesus and was saved.

When Jesus was on that cross dying, He was thinking of those lads. When Jesus breathed His Spirit into His disciples and went to be with the Father, He was thinking of those lads. When Jesus said, "I must go, so that the Comforter, Holy Spirit, can come and be everywhere", all the time He was thinking of those lads. When Jesus said we would do greater things, He was thinking of moments like these. The fact that these seven lads received the saving grace of their Saviour was because of Jesus. All the glory goes to Him. He didn't need me to do what He did to those guys, but He chose to work with and through me to accomplish His desire; firstly, because I took a risk, but secondly because He loves to bless His kids. This is particularly so when you step out with risk in faith, on the edge of making a complete fool of yourself. He honours great faith and the righteous prayer and declarations of His people, especially if it leads to getting one of His kids back. In Luke 15:7, Jesus says:

> *"What man among you, if he has a hundred sheep and loses one of them, does not leave the ninety-nine in the wilderness and go after the one which is lost, [searching] until he finds it? And when he has found it, he lays it on his shoulders, rejoicing. And when he gets home, he calls together his friends and his neighbours, saying to them, 'Rejoice with me, because I have found my lost sheep!' I tell you, in the same way there will be more joy in heaven over one sinner who repents than over ninety-nine righteous people who have no need of repentance."*

In closing I would ask you, "Are you ready to get the party started? It's never too late to become a world-changer from God's perspective. Is it your turn?" You are your next breath away from being found and set free. Jesus is waiting for you to turn and declare from your heart like I did, **"<u>SAVE ME RIGHT NOW, IN JESUS NAME!</u>"** As Frank said to me: "There is Power in the name of JESUS!"

When you are ready, declare this prayer and then find your nearest Christian friend or church, or seek me out on Facebook @ TheTattooedSaint,

"Dear Lord Jesus, I know that I am a sinner, and I ask for Your forgiveness. I believe You died for my sins and rose from the dead. I turn from my sins and invite You to come into my heart and life. I want to trust and follow You as my Lord and Saviour."

Why The Tattooed Saint?

Why have I called this book 'The Tattooed Saint', and why am I covered in tattoos? Firstly, it's God's book about my life and my life is tattooed on my body. Secondly, I was once covered in the stain of life. Now, I am covered in Scripture and images relating to God, because of what God first sealed in my heart. My tattoos are an extension of the same and my body, the temple of the Holy Spirit, glorifies God inwardly and outwardly! The Apostle Paul uses the word "Saint" many times in the Bible, and nearly always he is referring to Christians, not an individual or special Christian. I am not a sinner trying to be a Saint. I'm a Tattooed Saint trying not to sin, BY THE GRACE OF GOD AND THE POWER OF HIS SPIRIT AT WORK WITHIN ME.

Contact the author by emailing to
tattoedsaint7@gmail.com

INSPIRED TO WRITE A BOOK?

Contact

Maurice Wylie Media
Your Inspirational Publisher

Based in Northern Ireland and distributing around the world.
www.MauriceWylieMedia.com